International Series on Computer Entertainment and Media Technology

Series Editor

Newton Lee

The International Series on Computer Entertainment and Media Technology presents forward-looking ideas, cutting-edge research, and in-depth case studies across a wide spectrum of entertainment and media technology. The series covers a range of content from professional to academic. Entertainment Technology includes computer games, electronic toys, scenery fabrication, theatrical property, costume, lighting, sound, video, music, show control, animation, animatronics, interactive environments, computer simulation, visual effects, augmented reality, and virtual reality. Media Technology includes art media, print media, digital media, electronic media, big data, asset management, signal processing, data recording, data storage, data transmission, media psychology, wearable devices, robotics, and physical computing.

More information about this series at http://www.springer.com/series/13820

Krystina Madej

Interactivity, Collaboration, and Authoring in Social Media

 Springer

Krystina Madej
School of Literature, Media, and Communication
Georgia Institute of Technology
Atlanta, GA, USA

ISSN 2364-947X   ISSN 2364-9488   (electronic)
International Series on Computer Entertainment and Media Technology
ISBN 978-3-319-25950-5   ISBN 978-3-319-25952-9   (eBook)
DOI 10.1007/978-3-319-25952-9

Library of Congress Control Number: 2015953667

Springer Cham Heidelberg New York Dordrecht London

Printed on acid-free paper

Springer International Publishing AG Switzerland is part of Springer Science+Business Media (www.springer.com)

This book is dedicated to Mary Neilson and Douglas Grant, friends and colleagues with a love for ideas and conversation.

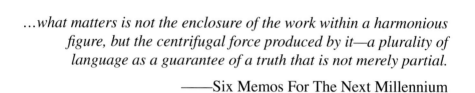

…what matters is not the enclosure of the work within a harmonious figure, but the centrifugal force produced by it—a plurality of language as a guarantee of a truth that is not merely partial.

——Six Memos For The Next Millennium
Italo Calvino

Prologue

Mission Statement

To uncover the lies and secrets being held from our Verona Citizens. To Speak the Absolute Truth. To Show the Facts and bring awareness to Verona. Verona Leaks is a non-for-profit organization, ferreting out all information withheld from public view. The goal is simple, if knowledge is power, then give the citizens back their power.

So begins the real story behind the untimely deaths of Romeo and Juliet.

Charged with bringing the real story behind the deaths of Romeo and Juliet to life through social media, students chose to work within a contemporary metaphor based on an organization noted for revealing facts, *WikiLeaks*. Three main sites document the extensive work students took on in their search to bring the truth to the public about the lives and events surrounding the ill-fated couple.

The City of Verona Speaks, the official city website, links readers to the individual *Facebook* sites of the main players (at http://projects.gnwc.ca/bp/).

VeronaLeaks, a *Wordpress* blog site, informs the citizens of Verona of information withheld from public view (at https://veronaleaks.wordpress.com).

The Indefatigable J. Murphy & Sons' website, the website of the firm of investigators hired by the City of Verona to look into organizational leaks and the deaths of Romeo and Juliet, provides information crucial to understanding the events that occurred (at https://jmurphyandsons.wordpress.com).

Acknowledgments

First, let me thank Richard Smith, the Director of the Center for Digital Media (CDM), who encouraged me to become involved in the narrative program at CDM, and to George Johnson, who graciously agreed to a co-taught class. They not only included me but also made me welcome at the center's innovative graduate program.

Thanks for the inspiration to use social media for retelling canonic stories go to Aaran Kashtan's students in the School of Literature, Media, and Communication (LMC) at Georgia Tech: Udita Menon and her team members Cassidy Burton, Cindy Huang, and Zac Zachow met the challenge of the project *The Future of the Book/The Book of the Future* with a Facebook adaptation of the Romeo and Juliet story.

I'm in particular debt to the grad students at CDM who responded with enthusiasm, creativity, and humor to writing *After Love Comes Destruction*. Thanks go to Nada Aljohani, Micheal Auger, Alan Correa, Patricia Nunez, Neshat Piroozan and in particular to Brett Pawson for his help in putting together documentation after the course was complete and for his penetrating views during our ongoing conversations about the process and product that resulted. Thanks go to Bill Zhao, who patiently responded to the team's technical hopes and needs, and to Mark Lange and Josh Miller, who ensured CDM's technology backed him fully.

A note of appreciation for encouragement to pursue publishing my research goes to Jay Telotte and Richard Utz, past and current chairs of my school, LMC, at Georgia Tech, who are inspiring in their dedication to spur the school's humanities scholars to communicate to their audiences.

Thank you to Margaret Walters, Sarah Robbins, and Susan Hunter (Director at the time) of the Masters of Professional Writing program at KSU who, through their courses, first kindled my interest in the evolution of narratives across media, the heteroglossia of language, and authors working collaboratively. Thanks in particular to Marjorie Luesebrink, whose vision of digital engagement has been a motivation to explore new possibilities since I first read her hypermedia novel *Califia* in 2001. Marjorie kindly accepted my invitation to speak at *ePublishing*, a conference I organized in 2003 for Robert Williams, Director of the KSU Library, on the impact of digital media on authors and libraries. She continues to inspire with her works and I'm grateful for her generosity. Thank you to Sue Thomas who I met at the second DAC conference (1999) where she explained the intent of trAce as a writer's resource and encouraged participation in the collaborative work *Noon Quilt*.

Thanks for many conversations about narrative and technology and how these intertwine to position literature within new media go to colleagues and professors at SFU: Paul Delany, Colette Colligan, and Leigh Davis of the Department of English and Jim Bizzocchi, John Bowen, Ron Wakkary, and Jim Budd of the School of Interactive Art and Technology. Particular thanks go to Douglas Grant, a dear colleague at SFU, who passed away in 2013. Douglas had a passion for learning, engaging with new ideas, and sharing his knowledge. His zest for spirited discussion about narrative, media, and the changing landscape of communication is greatly missed.

More recently, research into social media narrative brought me into contact with Rob Wittig, who kindly clarified details about his early work with *IN.S.OMNIA* and *Invisible Seattle*. I thank him for always taking the new road in writing social media narratives over a span of more than 30 years and generously and enthusiastically sharing his interest. Thanks to Ian Harper for contacting me many years ago about *Inanimate Alice*. I've followed Alice's life with interest. Thanks also for the assistance I've received from Ellen Rubin, John Lloyd Davies, Alastair O'Neill, Mark Bernstein, Julie Judkins, Christina Engelbart, Marty Ritchey, Ludovic Carpentier, and Richard Lowe in acquiring images that tell the story.

I'd like to thank my bookclub friends in Vancouver: Mary, Susan, Mary Jo, Grace, Kim, Alida, and Trish, for a personal view of a dedicated group of literature lovers and critics.

Thanks go to Marjorie Williams and Mary Neilson for their critical eye when reading early drafts and for suggestions for better ways to address a sentence or an idea.

I'm very grateful to the support of Newton Lee, who in 2003 published my first article on digital narrative in AMC's newly-minted Computers in Entertainment online magazine. Newton was my collaborator on *Disney Stories: Getting to Digital* and continues to encourage my research in digital narrative.

Thank you especially to my family for their patience with the many "later, later" activities which I will now have to catch up on.

Finally, thanks go to Courtney Clark and the many people at Springer Publishing who have helped to bring this book to digital and print life.

Contents

List of Figures

Part I
Interactive Narrative:
Collaborative Culture

When digital media is perceived only as a tool to deliver content the potential for using its affordances to explore meaning is lost. Rather than seeing media only as an access point, we can view it as a way to enhance the expressiveness of content. Today blogs, wikis, messaging, mash-ups, and social media (Facebook, Twitter, YouTube and others) offer authors ways to create narrative meaning that reflects our new media culture. We can look to the past for similarities and parallels to better understand how to use social media as a creative tool with which to dialogue, collaborate, and create interactive narratives.

(From Chap. 1)

Chapter 1
Introduction

Over the last few decades, digital technologies have inspired us to transform the narrative landscape.

Innovation and Change

At the forefront of narrative innovation are social media channels—speculative spaces for creating and experiencing stories that are interactive and collaborative. Unlike the print interactive fiction environment in which both authoring and reading are often solitary endeavors—the author creates the linked spaces, the reader works her/his way through them—social media offers a space that encourages collaboration. Unlike digital interactive fiction environments in which readers create their stories within an already structured world, social media offers an open-ended environment in which readers can keystroke plotlines and together with colleagues and friends, as well as with strangers, create stories.

Early communications avenues such as email and discussion forums, the precursors of social media, had already set a paradigm of dialogue and sharing for computer users by the 1990s. Some of the earliest users of these communication avenues were the developers of text adventures such as *Adventure* and *Zork*, who were part of the university research community and for whom these tools were part of the day-to-day work environment. Early enthusiasts took advantage of the communication capacity of their computer networks to discuss adventure narratives and games and these communities of users grew as the genres evolved.

During the late 1970s and early 1980s the Internet was used successfully for information exchange and discussion within academic, research, and special interest communities. Subscription services such as *Compuserve* in the 1980s brought channels for online participation to the general public. With the development of the WWW and the introduction of graphical browsers in the early 1990s the potential for the general public to use the internet as a space for working collaboratively burgeoned. Before the WWW, hypertext and hypermedia narratives, which grew

© The Author(s) 2016
K. Madej, *Interactivity, Collaboration, and Authoring in Social Media*,
International Series on Computer Entertainment and Media Technology,
DOI 10.1007/978-3-319-25952-9_1

alongside adventure games and RPGs, were distributed to the public first via diskettes and then CD-ROMs for use on personal computers, and soon after through online subscription services such as Compuserve and *America Online (AOL)*. Writing applications that were specific to authors working in digital media were just being developed in the 1980s. When the application *Storyspace* was introduced to the public in 1986 by the publisher Eastgate, it finally gave authors who weren't tech savvy a simple tool for writing hypertext. The year after, 1987, *HyperCard,* released for the Macintosh and AppleIIGS, offered a way to include different media in their stories. Then with the introduction of the *Mosaic* browser in 1992 and *Netscape Navigator* in 1993–1994 hypermedia moved beyond the sphere of special interest groups into the general community where it was quickly embraced.

Interactive narrative and collaborative authoring in their current expression in social media have many antecedents. Early written texts such as the Ancient Greek epic *The Iliad,* although assigned to one author, Homer, were a collection of stories that had been passed down orally for centuries. Combinatory systems for poetry and divination that added interactivity and collaboration as dimensions of the narrative experience were used as early as the fourth century. Text-generating interactive devices such as volvelles that required a participatory effort to produce a final narrative were introduced into the manuscript tradition in Europe in the thirteenth century. Volvelles, together with lift-the-flap images, transitioned successfully to printed texts in the fifteenth century. In the eighteenth century manipulables such as harlequinades gave readers choices for sequencing through text and collaborating on creating their own version of a story. In the nineteenth century narratives such as *The History and Adventures of Little Henry* included paper figures that could be used by readers to act out their own version of a story. Over the centuries authors have taken advantage of each new media to give readers opportunities for tangible collaboration in the creation of a story by designing the narrative experience to be physically as well as cognitively interactive (Cramer 2000; Karr 2004; Helfand 2006; Gravelle et al. 2012).

An advantage of living within a contemporary Web world is that our experiences with computers and digital environments provide a new backdrop against which to position how humans have interacted with narrative in the past. Sherry Turkle tells us that working with computers has changed our habits of mind and our conception of thinking, knowing, understanding, and creating (Turkle 2004). The way we conceive the present changes our perception of the past; the influences around us invariably shift our viewpoint so that we see the past texts in new ways (Borges 1962). When combinatorials and manipulables are viewed in light of the current interest authors have in creating interactive narrative experiences (hypertexts, hypermedia, narrative games, twitter novels) it becomes apparent that a trajectory of interest exists throughout our narrative history for including readers as participants in story creation and providing the tools necessary to do so.

When digital media is perceived only as a tool to deliver content the potential for using its affordances to explore meaning is lost. Rather than seeing media only as an access point, we can view it as a way to enhance the expressiveness of content.

Today blogs, wikis, messaging, mash-ups, and social media (*Facebook, Twitter, YouTube* and others) offer authors ways to create narrative meaning that reflects our new media culture. We can look to the past for similarities and parallels to better understand how to use social media as a creative tool with which to dialogue, collaborate, and create interactive narratives.

The purpose of this book is to explore the opportunities for engagement provided by forms of narrative that embrace interactivity and collaborative authoring. The approach taken is to consider narrative as material culture, that is, narrative is interpreted as a physical representation of knowledge as it is constructed through a culture's practice of discourse. In Part I, the book prospects the last millennium for antecedents of today's authoring practices. Chapter 1 introduces the long tradition of interactivity and collaboration in creating narratives and how these narratives have throughout the centuries constructed new knowledge through a process that includes dialogism, agency, and collaboration. Chapter 2 takes the reader from the philosophy of Socrates regarding the written word to multi-ended choose your own adventure books. Chapter 3 takes the review of interactive and collaborative narrative into the digital world and provides an overview of the symbiotic evolution of narrative and digital technology from the mid-1960s until today. It does so with a view to considering how today's digital manifestations are a continuation, perhaps an iteration, perhaps a novel pioneering of humans' abiding interest in narrative. Chapter 4 looks at the evolution of social media and its interrelation with authoring both personal and fictive narratives.

In light of social media's ability to act as both authoring vehicle and delivery mechanism and the apparent public interest in participating as both author and reader through/in this media environment, the two roles of author and reader have never before been juxtaposed more effectively or been more complicit. In Part II the book presents the process of creating an interactive and collaborative narrative through the affordances of social media. The narrative is Shakespeare's story *Romeo and Juliet*, the circumstance is a remediation of the story by a group of graduate students. The case study deconstructs the collaborative authoring process and shows how a generative narrative space evolved around the authors' use of media in ways they had not previously considered both for authoring and for delivery of the final narrative object. The resulting interactive narrative demonstrates that a social media environment facilitates a meaningful and productive collaborative authorial experience with an interactive narrative that has an abundance of networked, personally expressive, and visually and textually referential content as a result.

Defining the Terms

In this paper **material culture** is the physical evidence (artifacts, objects) that defines our society and culture; **dialogue** is two-way communication in which participants influence the content and form of the discourse; **interactivity** is reciprocal action that prompts dialogue and collaboration with a tangible artifact or a person; **agency** is the capacity of the reader to have a choice in their behavior; **collaboration** is participation in a dialogic process by authors and/or readers, for the purpose of creating an artifact; **narrative** is either expository, which provides information, or literary, which tells a story; and **story** is all the events of a narrative in sequence with **plot** being the way these events are presented.

The following sections further define material culture, agency, and collaboration, and the narrative elements content, form, and media.

Material Culture

Humans construct their knowledge of the world as schemata, short bits of story that, with time, build towards a narrative perspective from which we view the world. The psychologist Frederic Bartlett introduced the concept of schema in 1932 when conducting work on constructivist memory; he described a schema as "an active organization of past reactions, or of past experience" (Bartlett, p. 201). Bartlett understood cognition as working top down with sets of culturally-contextualized information imbedded in long term memory that help people structure their immediate reality by being there in the background, like a backstory, always on call. He saw schemata as dynamic and being added to or changed each time they were referenced, or anything connected to them was referenced. Schemas exist in the background accumulating and adding depth and breadth to each new experience.

Humans first used their voices and their gestures to share their narratives. Since the days of drawing on cave walls they have put to use the materials within their grasp to give their stories material presence. The historical or archaeological artifacts we find and examine reflect a fixed moment that represents both what has happened before and what is about to happen (Gombrich 1964). These artifacts are a result of an ongoing process of dialogue and growth within the culture and reflect only a moment in time, a thin slice of our culture's narrative schemata as it has continuously evolved.

Humans have the uncanny ability not only to use what they have at hand as a way to manifest their stories, not just to respond to a medium, but to use the medium innovatively, improve it, and help it change. As each subsequent generation actualizes anew the stories that represent the culture's thoughts and deeds, every work of narrative gives voice to this changing expression. Narratives in digital media continue the process of evolution far more rapidly than do the media of the past: each narrative creation is quickly overwhelmed by a new manifestation as we move forward eagerly and respond with alacrity to the changes in our media.

In *Ethnography and Material Culture* the British archaeologist Christopher Tilley suggests that the meaning of an object is created when a group uses it for a purpose. "Meaning is created out of situated contextualized social action which is in continuous dialectical relationship with generative rule-based structures forming both a medium for and an outcome of action" (Tilley, p. 260). Because narrative has long been a way humans create meaning for themselves as a society or culture, it is implicit in the practice of sharing, collaborating, and communicating within a culture. Narratives help us link facts, make them our own, and dialogue with others. It is the mechanism society has used and continues to use to relate emotions, thoughts, and ideas that reflect the values of its culture.

As *material culture* narrative can be studied and defined as content represented by a form within a medium. Throughout history humans have continuously invented new material ways to tell their stories and have represented their ideas with rich narrative, technical precision, and strong aesthetic design. Our stories have been painted on cave walls, carved into stone, written on papyrus, shaped in pottery, laid in mosaics; they have been recited by orators, sung by bards, performed by mimes, puppeteers and troupes; they have been printed in books, transported over telephone lines, and sent by radio waves; they have been carried on celluloid film, captured by cathode ray tubes for television, honored in museums, and enacted in entertainment parks. The virtual environments of computers, gaming systems, and personal devices, such as smart phones, are only the latest iteration of a communication paradigm for our narrative-based culture. As we uncover our 40,000+ years of narrative, these artifacts provide an ample supply of material culture upon which we can reflect to gain understanding of the way in which we tell and receive stories *today*.

When we reflect on our human narratives as material culture and view our current approach to creating narrative artifacts in light of historical examples, we are provided with references for analysis and interpretation. Viewing narrative in historical context broadens and deepens our perspective. When we understand how narratives have been used in the past to communicate facts, ideas, and points of view, we can consider more objectively the way they are used today. We can also conjecture more knowledgeably about the future of narrative transformation in evolving formats such as social media in digital environments.

Not only does the historical context of material culture benefit narrative analysis it can also act as a driver for the *creation* of new narratives. Arguments about the paramountcy of such traditional notions as narrative arc and linearity, and Freytag's triangle and climax, disappear under the weight of historical examples that contradict these limiting views of narrative and open up the horizon. To some however, historical understanding of the traditions of narrative is an impediment to innovation and creativity. In *The Rise of the Novel,* Ian Watt provides one critics views on the evolution of literary innovation: "It is only from the ignorant that we can now have anything original; every master copies from those that are of established authority, and does not look at the natural object" (Watt, p. 58). In this view, lack of knowledge in an era rampant with knowledge is seen as the only breeding ground for new ideas. This book's perspective differs and suggests that knowledge of past diversities in expression will foster less repetition and more experimentation with new forms and media.

Content, Form, and Medium

The elements that constitute a narrative and engage us are consistently the same whether the narrative appears as a manuscript, a printed book, a harlequinade, or a contemporary blog fiction. The narrative artifact, as a schema, consists of:

- content—what is of value to share
- form—the symbols used to share
- medium—the means for sharing

Each of these elements is an integral part of the actualized narrative. Each can be investigated individually, however, the elements are interdependent and function symbiotically; in analyzing any one of them, the others must be given due consideration.

Narrative material culture dates back millennia. While these categories are consistent over time, the manifestation of each element changes in tandem with the political and social influences and the technological advances of each era. We can consider the whole the schema, and each of these elements a set of scripts which necessarily change with each era. Whether the narrative artifact is expository and informs about facts, or literary and tells a story about human nature, each of the scripts represents a *moment in time*. The "captured narrative moment has absorbed and reflects the light of human experience"[1] and each has been imprinted with the values of its era. As an example let us take the evolution of computers from 1960 to today.

Content: what is of value to share
    1960: numbers and data of value to business, institutions, and government
    2010: extensive range of data including personal expression

Form: symbols used to share
    1960: protocols for punch card input and output
    2010: text, image, sound, video, and AR programs

Media: means for sharing
    1960: main frame computers that host data
    2010: any device that can host digital data (PCs, tablets, mobiles, AR devices, etc.)
    and can be used to share this data (Fig. 1.1)

These elements provide a simple framework for examining past and present narrative. For example, in the poetic volvelle *Denckring*, units of language were the *content* that took the *form* of text combinations produced by interacting with the five disks of the volvelle, the *media*. Between the thirteenth and the seventeenth century volvelles evolved to accommodate poetic content. In today's social media microblog Twitter, personal *content* takes the *form* of a 140-character tweet that is posted through the *media* application Twitter. Since 2006 Twitter has changed to

---

[1] Marjorie Williams, email to author March 2015.

Fig. 1.1 From the Fortran punch card in 1960 to the smart mobile device in 2015—changing narrative technologies

accommodate content such as photos and tall tweets. Such adjustments reflect narrative's responsiveness to evolving interests and technologies in a culture and modify our perception of narrative.

Dialogism

A material narrative artifact is the result of humans' desire to communicate and their use of the language and media of the time to do so. Russian literary theorist Mikhail Bakhtin (1895–1975) believed that "language is not an abstract system of normative forms but rather a concrete heteroglot conception of the world" (Morson and Emerson 1990). The most important feature of narrative or "human utterance," as Bakhtin called it, is that narrative is dialogic—that a constant dialogue exists between past and current authors, and then, as ideas are instantiated as text, with current and future readers. Utterances do not exist in a vacuum, but are freighted with past meanings and contexts as well as current meanings and contexts. Each utterance first has the historical context of the word as the author has chosen it—every word has its own linguistic archaeology, with hidden strata of historical uses and reiterative connotatons. It then becomes a social construct as it has the life shaped by the dialogue the author has with his audience within a contemporary context.

Julia Kristeva, who introduced Bakhtin's work through her translations and interpretations in the late 1970s, used the term "intertextual" for the idea of dialogism; that term gave a preferred status to text. Dialogue, however, is ongoing amongst all content, forms, and media (Durey 1991).

As a precept of dialogism Bakhtin believed that the cultural world consists of both centripetal and centrifugal forces. Centripetal forces seek to impose order on what is an essentially heterogeneous and messy world: while centrifugal forces either purposefully or for no particular reason continually disrupt that order. Bakhtin called the linguistic forces and what resulted because of them heteroglossia.

All language and culture is made of many small and unsystematic alterations. While centralizing tendencies (from associations, governments, schools, dictionaries, etymologies) aim to shape a language, decentralizing tendencies (local culture, street language, folk sayings, anecdotes) disrupt that order. Incremental changes add up until they are no longer incremental but are sufficient to be visible. Each new narrative artifact reflects the changes that have occurred since the previous narrative instantiation. In contrast to the past, in today's digital media these incremental changes give rise to and make visible new genres very quickly.

Agency

While narrative consists of content, form, and medium that is a result of a continuous dialogue within the culture, it is enabled through engagement that provides for agency. The Oxford Dictionary tells us that agency derives from the medieval Latin agentia, from agent or 'doing,' and arrived in the English language in the mid-seventeenth century. It defines agency as "a thing or person that acts to produce a particular result." Narrative artifacts are not isolated objects, standing on their own; they "act" on humans and affect behavior—they both have agency and provide agency to readers.

Within today's literary tradition, agency is a function of narrative's content rather than of its form. Content is seen to have the ability to evoke a response or a change in readers; readers in turn have the agency to construct the narrative for themselves (Bruner 2004). Within the archeological tradition, archeologists see the actual artifact (the form together with the medium) as being given agency by those who created it.

The discussion on agency ranges greatly. At one end, Janet Hoskins tells us in her work *Agency, Biography and Objects* that objects are intended to act upon humans or they wouldn't be created, and as such have an innate agency (Hoskins 2006). At the other end, Carl Knappett argues in *Thinking Through Material Culture: An Interdisciplinary Perspective,* that, as they are not alive, objects cannot have real agency, rather theirs is a secondary effect caused through the connection with those who create them and those who engage with them (Knappet 2005). There is consensus, however, that humans imbue objects with purpose, that the intent is for the object to effect, if not a change, then a response, and that the lasting effect or legacy of the object and its purpose is dependent on engagement (Russo 2007).

Accepting narrative as material culture draws together agency of content with agency as represented in the actual artifact. Content and form, together with the medium through which humans engage with narrative comprise agency on multiple levels. When interactive narratives in past centuries provided an opportunity for physical interaction with narrative content, agency shifted to include somatic or embodied agency along with cognitive agency. As readers dressed a *Little Henry* paper doll in rags after he'd fallen from grace in *The History and Adventures of Little Henry,* they gave tangible presence to the text because they could physically enact the story as it was written. Agency is more apparent in such physically engaging activities than it is with the reading of text narratives when it is solely a cognitive activity. In today's world of blog fiction agency results from the reader's participation as author both of content and of the physical construction of the narrative. In Twitter fiction, for instance, the reader adds to the story by tweeting the next sentence: both a cognitive and a physical act.

Collaboration

Collaboration is the action of working with someone to produce or create something. Collaboration in narrative is often taken to mean creating content—i.e. two or more authors collaborate to write a book together. Authors go through a personal internal process when writing. They hold an internal dialogue: about ideas for different scenarios, about their characters, about scene settings. During collaboration this internal process is made external and the dialogue then includes another author or authors. That which was internal and personal becomes external and a conversation with someone. More than a conversation, however, is required to make the effort collaborative. The conversations of collaboration are a two-way process: they include listening and responding, collecting and recollecting, and, then adjusting thinking to include new information. Authors work *together* to *socially* construct knowledge from their *combined* experiences.

Writing collaboratively requires a willingness to acknowledge the value of others' experiences in creating knowledge; it requires sharing knowledge in a two-way exchange of experiences; and it requires accommodating other, often very different experiences, both in the creation process and in the end artifact. Such a process requires that the participants understand and accept that conversations are co-constructed and that the knowledge or narrative artifact that is the end goal is more than an accumulation of facts stacked upon each other. The collaborative process requires integrating others' perspectives to make new meaning. Conversations will include not only ideas about content, but also emotions, behaviors, and approaches that will influence the process as well as the end artifact.

Collaboration does not come easily to everyone. To build a collaborative culture participants need to define and build a shared purpose and then make a combined effort to reach that purpose. They need to create an environment that allows each one to work flexibly, so they can add their own nuances to the project, yet have a sufficiently disciplined framework to guide the project to completion. As part of a collaborative effort participants need to cultivate an ethic of contribution, to view collaboration as valued, and to appropriately reward it (Adler et al. 2011).

Narrative is not only content however. It consists of content, form, and medium, and collaboration can be realized across all three of these elements of narrative. In print texts, for instance, content may be authored by one individual but is often edited by another. The narrative form is then produced by a team that consists of typesetters, designers, and line editors, among others, who, while largely invisible, must function as an efficient and effective collaborative unit to produce the final artifact within its medium, the print book. Similar processes function across all media. In digital media additional opportunities for taking different paths to produce and deliver narratives have evolved, both for collaborative teams and for individual effort. Collaborative teams that produce narrative games, augmented reality narratives, and crowd-sourced fiction include spontaneous participation by players/ readers who act as producers of content and form. Individual authors benefit from computer technologies that have been efficiently developed to provide support for composing and publish digital narrative themselves, whether desktop published books or Twitterfiction.

It is here that the collaborative nature of the reader's relationship with the text and the reader as author must be mentioned. While Bakhtin's theories of dialogism compulsorily implicated the reader together with the author in the creation of the narrative, Roland Barthes, in *Death of the Author*, gave the reader more responsibility for giving the narrative its essential meaning. For both, the narrative as scripted[2] could not have a single interpretation and took on a new meaning with each new reader. For Barthes, it was the reader who imposed upon the narrative his/her own impressions and understandings; there was no need for the author's meaning to be interpreted. Barthes also theorized that the narrative constitutes "a multi-dimensional space" which must be disentangled and not interpreted (Barthes 1997). In this he prefigured the networked and multimodal approach to narrative that has evolved in digital space. Can Bakhtin's dialogism and Barthes' disentanglement process be considered collaboration between the reader and author in one case and the reader and the text in the other? In that the narrative is co-constructed, certainly. This is a passive collaboration, resulting more from happenstance than planning.

A collective effort is a collaboration of a certain kind. Collective authoring is a feature of networked and crowd sourced narrative, forms of narrative based in blogging and microblogging in which writers' contributions are turn-based and sequential. If the end product is to be a narrative artifact with a traditional form (short story, play, novel) then editing of the contributions needs to happen either along the way or at the end of the collective period. Editing is done by an individual or by a team, but not usually by everyone who has contributed text. The dialogue which is part of the collaborative process between authors is not a factor in sequenced narratives until and if editing is done by a team. From a macro view the process is a collective one, from a micro view, each author has a relationship with the text but not necessarily a collaborative relationship with the other authors.

The process of collaboration can be viewed from different perspectives and have different nuances and there is a challenge in determining what scenarios collaborative authoring might include. Narratives are social constructs shaped by the relationship between author and reader, by context, and by the media through which they are

---

[2] Barthes uses "scripted" rather than "authored" to remove the semblance of authority given to the writer of a text.

presented. Collaboration in creating narrative can be passive or active, cognitive or somatic, and be between author and reader, reader and text, author and author, or among multiple authors. Constructing narrative requires more than one collaborative scenario:

- author and author
    collaboration between or among authors to create new literary works
- author and past authors and texts—dialogism and intertextuality
    collaboration between author and all past authors of the text, and the author and their environment that creates meaning which is contextual. This can be a passive as well as active process on the part of the author.
- reader and text
    reader's cognitive participation in the dialogic process, a collaboration in which the reader's personal context is implicated and creates a different meaning and narrative for each reader
- reader and interactive text
    collaboration of the reader with a narrative artifact in which they create new information passively, based completely in the data provided (as in a volvelle)
- reader and tangible interactive text
    collaboration of the reader with a narrative artifact in which they follow a path among many offered to co-create a scripted story
- reader and emergent text
    collaboration of the reader with a narrative artifact to which they add new texts/events that change the course of the story and possibly the ending
- networked authors (collective + collaborative)
    collaboration among a group of authors to collect texts which are edited by individuals or a team of editors or authors
- crowd sourced authors (collective + collaborative)
    collection from many writers of texts which are edited by individuals or a team of editors or authors

These scenarios apply in varying degrees to the construction of narrative artifacts. The next chapter begins a look at the past into the inventive ways people have found to engage interactively with narrative artifacts to tell stories, and how they do so collaboratively.

Chapter 2
Print Narrative, Interactivity, and Collaboration

All storytelling begins with a conversation

Narrative and Knowledge

Stories are a way to share ideas and create meaning. Today, the intellectual involvement with content is often mediated by physical engagement with the narrative artifact, sometimes the printed pages of a book, sometimes the pixilated screen of a personal computer. There is a difference between engaging with a story through a material artifact as we do today, and engaging with it orally, as was done for millennia before written stories became common. This difference is our starting point for discussing interactivity and collaboration in narrative as it has evolved since the first days of the codex.[1]

Literary tradition as we know it in Western Society came to us in its first written representation as the epic of Classic Greek civilization (around 800 BCE). Although presented through the voice of Homer, the *Iliad*, and subsequently the *Odyssey*, were a compilation of stories that had been passed down within the oral tradition of Greek culture, a tradition of collective authorship (Whitman 1958). The newly evolved written text, however, had its detractors. In *Orality and Literacy* Walter Ong discussed the changes that the shift from orality to literacy caused in various societies. He presented the philosopher Socrates' beliefs (circa 400 BCE) that writing was not a good vehicle for dialogue, which he saw as critical to humanity. For Socrates, writing was a dead medium; it reified ideas. That is, it set ideas in concrete text that was immutable (Ong 2002).

---

[1] The codex was the first book artifact. It consisted of sheets of papyrus or parchment, bound together, and protected with a cover. It had replaced the scroll as the common form used for narrative by about 600 CE.

© The Author(s) 2016
K. Madej, *Interactivity, Collaboration, and Authoring in Social Media*,
International Series on Computer Entertainment and Media Technology,
DOI 10.1007/978-3-319-25952-9_2

Socrates did not write down his ideas. They were brought to us through the writings of the philosopher Plato, one of his students. In the dialogue *Phaedrus* (circa 370 BCE) Plato had Socrates discussing with his disciple Phaedrus the idea that knowledge could only be attained and conveyed through back and forth oral dialogue. *Written* words were not able to defend themselves through dialogue (Cooper 1997).

From Socrates' perspective, writing was knowledge communication rather than knowledge creation; only oral discourse could convey man's true intellectual participation in making knowledge. "Reading mere words, in his mind, is akin to looking at a lake rather than swimming in it—or worse, looking at a lake and thinking that now you know *how* to swim."[2] Socrates implied that humans fooled themselves if they believed that writing could replace oral dialogue and represent their finest ideas (Ong 2002).

In orality, discourse is dynamic—humans speak with each other and have the opportunity to respond immediately. As an ideal, such a dynamic exchange is difficult to achieve when the interface used is a narrative artifact such as a manuscript or print text, which seems at first glance to be mute. The value given to dialogue and exchange as a means of knowledge creation provoked those who produced and used written materials to find ways to present ongoing discussion. In medieval times *glossae ordinariae*, comments on content, were included in new versions of texts and provided evidence of the dialogue between scholars. Manuscripts, and later printed books, were published with commentary added to, first, the original text and, subsequently, to texts that incorporated previously made comments. The contents of the manuscripts would evolve with each new copying.

In *Decretals of Gregory*, a thirteenth century manuscript of biblical commentary (Fig. 2.1), we see an example of the juxtaposition of original text and subsequent commentary made by different scholars. The discussion surrounding the content of the written page is, if not dynamic, visible. Scholars also made notations for themselves in the margins of manuscripts (marginalia), which provided a further exchange of thoughts as these manuscripts were shared among scholars. A very common format for this period, the *glossae ordinariae* showed that human ingenuity could prevail over limitations a medium might initially seem to have. The manuscript as narrative artifact had become a site of both communication and exchange: it did not only pass on knowledge but endeavored to create it.

---

[2] Cartoonist and designer David Malki on writing http://wondermark.com/socrates-vs-writing/.

Fig. 2.1 *Decretals of Gregory* shows both *glossae ordinariae* and marginalia. Circa 1241

The First Computers

Even before moveable type brought readers mass production, authors were pushing the boundaries of the codex. The dialogue between author and reader was made tangible when in thirteenth century Europe manuscripts began to include manipulable devices in their texts.[3] These included as simple a device as a sundial illustrated on a page on which a reader could place a stylus to ascertain the time, to complex combinatory devices such as volvelles. Volvelles consisted of one or more graduated or shaped paper disks sewn together within the manuscript that readers could manipulate to align information "geometrically as matrices; relationally, as concepts; and idealogically, as radical new paradigms for interdisciplinary thinking" (Helfand 2006).

The first volvelle that has been found in a European manuscript was designed by Matthew Paris, a Benedictine monk. Paris included the volvelle, a simple disk that determined the changing lunar date of Easter, in his *Chronica Majora* (circa 1250). Much more complex were the volvelles designed by Ramon Llull for his *Ars Magna* (*The Great Art*, circa 1305). Llull was a prominent and prolific Majorcan

---

[3] Volvelles were first used in Arabic writings around 1000 CE (Turner 1992).

writer, philosopher, and scientist of the thirteenth and fourteenth centuries (Gravelle et al. 2012). At a time when writers in Europe were beginning to create narratives in the vernacular, he is noted for writing the first major work of prose fiction, *Blanquer*, in Catalan (Doody 1997). At 33, Llull underwent an epiphany and became a Third Order Franciscan. With the purpose of using logic and reason to persuade Muslims to the Christian faith, he developed a method that combined religious and philosophical ideas to create new paths of insight and combine elements of thinking (as evidenced by words and phrases) to logically construct "proofs of God." He fashioned a series of mechanical devices that used as content the classification system he had devised to categorize everything in nature into a higher and lower order and attributes of God as he had defined them. The *Ars Magna* provided four devices that recombined letters or terms strictly defined according to his classification system. The last of the four devices was a volvelle that consisted of three moveable disks. Llull believed that by manipulating the disks and combining words to create statements, a higher knowledge would be revealed and would provide logical answers to questions about religion and creation (Dalakov 2015). Llull's purpose was not to reproduce knowledge that existed but to investigate truths, instigate new ways of thinking, and produce new proofs through these combinatory devices. His expectation was that individuals who had access to his manuscripts would interact with the devices included, collaborate in creating knowledge, and be swayed in their convictions by the logical proofs that the combinatory devices provided (Zweig 1997).

Figure 2.2 shows *Figure One* from the four figures in Llull's *Ars Magna*. Each level of the volvelle represents one segment of a sentence, which, when combined, stated an irrefutable religious or theological truth. Also shown is *Figure Four*, the volvelle, as it was included in the manuscript.

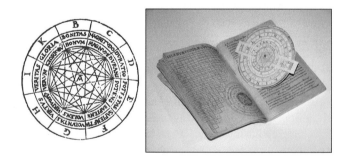

Fig. 2.2 Ramon Llull's *Figure One* and the *Ars Magna* open on *Figure Four*. 1305 CE

Figure 2.3 shows the terms used in the *Four Figures*. When combined *Figure One* terms identified absolute principles—'Wisdom is Power.' *Figure Two* terms identified relative principles—'Angels are different from elements.' *Figure Three* terms provided questions: 'Where is virtue final?' *Figure Four* terms generated complex propositions and questions.

	Absolute principles	Relative principles	Questions	Subjects	Virtues	Vices
B	Goodness	Difference	Whether	God	Justice	Avarice
C	Greatness	Concord	What	Angel	Prudence	Gluttony
D	Eternity	Opposition	Whence	Heaven	Fortitude	Luxury
E	Power	Priority	Which	Man	Temperance	Pride
F	Wisdom	Centrality	How many	Imaginative	Faith	Sloth
G	Will	Finality	What kind	Sensitive	Hope	Envy
H	Virtue	Majority	When	Vegetative	Charity	Anger
I	Truth	Equality	Where	Elemental	Patience	Untruthfulness
K	Glory	Minority	How/with what	Instrumental	Piety	Inconstancy

Fig. 2.3 Letters and attributes used in Llull's *Four Figures*

The importance Llull placed on using dialogue and collaboration was demonstrated in his use of interactive elements in both the *Ars Magna* and the *Ars Brevis*, as well as by depictions of himself and his leading disciple, Thomas le Myésier, in the midst of discussions they had. Their dialogue was visualized in the miniature illustrations in the *Electorium Parvum Seu Breviculum*, a fourteenth century compilation of Llull's writings, one of which is shown in Fig. 2.4.

Fig. 2.4 Ramon Llull and Thomas le Myesier in discussion. Circa 1321

Because of their precision, volvelles came to be used extensively in architecture, astronomy, navigation, and mathematics to calculate or compute data. In the Middle Ages these knowledge areas were inextricably bound up with philosophy, religion/ theology, and mysticism. Until the seventeenth century, truth and realism were not the "verite humaine" of the enlightenment or the "concrete objects of sense-perception" of today, instead they were universals or abstractions based in religious beliefs (Watt 1957, pp. 10–11). People did not yet look to their own interpretation but rather to interpretations provided by higher authorities. When using volvelles, readers engaged with authoritative text through a dynamic delivery system. We can view their engagement as collaborative authoring that allowed them to create new knowledge and a new narrative that was yet based in acceptable universal ideas. These devices were the analog computers of their day and provided their users with a collaborative and interactive narrative experience. Such a dynamic use of text might have convinced even Socrates that writing was not "dead" and immutable but could be used as a dialogue to create knowledge, not simply to represent it.

The use of tangible interactive devices persisted and increased when mass-produced print was brought to Europe in the early 1450s with Johannes Gutenberg's introduction of moveable type. The first print volvelle was included in Johannes Mueller's *Kalendar* (1474, Nuremberg) to compute events such as eclipses and position of the sun and moon.[4] Until the 1600s volvelles gave readers the opportunity to interact with expository texts. In 1651 Georg Philipp Harsdörffer created a poetic volvelle, the *Denckring or Five-fold Thought-ring*. First printed in his *Poetischer Trichter* (*Poet's Funnel*), this device was made of five paper discs each inscribed with units of language along its edge that could be combined to create "97,209,600 combinations" (Trettien 2010).[5]

Fig. 2.5 Harsdörffer used five nested rings in the poetic *Denckring*

---

[4] A digital edition of *The Arte of Navigation* (1584) that allows readers to construct the images in the book is available online at http://plato.acadiau.ca/courses/engl/rcunningham/digitaltext/index.html.

[5] See Trettien's *Ars Combinatoria* for more photos of Harsdörffer's poetic volvelle. http://www.whitneyannetrettien.com/arscombinatoria/.

As the disks were spun, they produced text and generated meaning for Harsdörffer. Figure 2.5 shows the *Denckring*. In each of the four corners are illustrations of hands that indicate the physical interaction through which the artifact engaged the reader. Harsdörffer was continuing a tradition of combinatory poetry that had existed since the Centos of the third century. Poets borrowed segments of other poets work and combined them to make a new work, or a Cento, of their own. Centos were governed by rules laid down around 350 CE. One such rule stated that Centos were to be made completely of segments of other poets work (Palmieri 2012).[6] The author collaborated with other poets through their poetry to create new work.

In addition to volvelles, manuscripts and printed books included lift-the-flap images called moveables. These flaps were used to show before and after scenes, to view human anatomy, and to complete diagrams. A typical example of the use of moveables is in Johan Stoeffler's treatises on mathematics, astronomy, and astrology, *Elucidatio Fabricae Ususque Astrolabii* (1524), a standard work used by astronomers and surveyors for many years.[7] Figure 2.6 shows an image of an astrolabe, an early computer used to make astronomical measurements before the development of the sextant. It consisted of a disk with the edge marked in degrees and a pivoted pointer. The fold-out sections were used to make it easier to understand the circles and lines bound by the astrolabe.

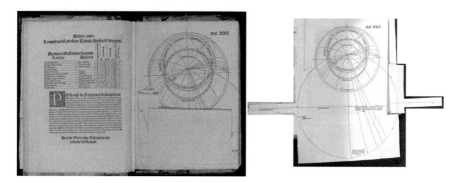

Fig. 2.6 Sixteenth century lift-the-flap image of an astrolabe by Johan Stoeffler

The artist Pietro Bertelli was a vanguard of socially inspired, rather than scientific or mystical, interactive images/texts. Working in Venice, which was noted for its opulently dressed courtesans, he created a number of works that reflected courtesan culture. *Cortigiana Veneza*—Venetian Courtesan, from *Diversarum Nationum Habitus* (1591), shown in Fig. 2.7, has a lift-the-flap of the gown skirt that reveals the courtesan wearing man-style breeches and the extremely high footwear

---

[6] A reconstruction of combinatory poems written as early as 330 can be found on the Florian Cramer's website *Permutations*. http://permutations.pleintekst.nl.

[7] The entire Elucidatio Fabricae Ususque Astrolabii can be found at https://books.google.com/books?id=__E5AAAAcAAJ&hl=en.

(calcagnini)[8] of the era. Readers could engage, if and when they chose to, with this daring reveal, and in a new and intimate way participate through personal interaction to co-construct the visual narrative about courtesans. These works were at the leading edge of the tangible interactivity that would become very popular in print narrative in the next centuries.

Fig. 2.7 *Cortigiana Veneza* lift-the-flap by Pietro Bertelli. Circa 1591

Tangible Narrative

Interactive or moveable devices used to enhance and make tangible *literary* narratives became popular at the end of the 1700s. Named metamorphoses, mechanicals, harlequinades, transformations, and turned-up books, these narrative devices took a number of different forms. All included some kind of device that could be opened or moved by the reader or that transformed when a page was opened. Some devices were simple, others consisted of intricately cut and complex structures.

Harlequinades were first created in 1765 by the printer Robert Sayer. Sayer, inspired by the pantomimes of the day, wanted to show stories in a series of changing scenes that emulated a performance. The harlequinade was printed on one sheet that was cut and folded into flaps rather than pages. It could be opened and closed to reveal images and text in various combinations and lead readers through a sequence

---

[8] Information on Calcagnini can be found at http://irenebrination.typepad.com/irenebrination_notes_on_a/2013/06/calcagnini-palazzo-mocenigo.html.

of scenes that told the story. Figure 2.8 shows a harlequinade of a play popular at the time, *Queen Mab* (Madej 2002). It consists of four pages each of which has two attached flaps. Each section illustrates in sequence one of the 12 six-line stanzas of the poem used as text. Readers unfolded the story by raising or lowering the flaps. They could follow the sequence of the text or could open the flaps randomly, which provided an unusual juxtaposition of sequences. The dialogue between reader and text was made tangible when the reader physically manipulated the flaps and collaborated in enacting the cause and effect that moved the sequences forward.

Fig. 2.8 *Queen Mab* or *The Tricks of Harlequin*, #6, Robert Sayer, 1771

In the early 1700s, books, including moveables, were still primarily published for adults. As is the case with some books today, the line between adult and children's literature was often blurred. Many adult stories, such as *Robinson Crusoe*, were adopted by children as their own; many fairytales were considered suitable reading material to be enjoyed by adults. As childrens' book publishing was more vigorously pursued after the mid-1700s, more books that had moveable parts were created for them. This was in keeping with progressive notions promoted by John Locke in *Some Thoughts on Education* (1692). Locke believed that children needed to enjoy and to be actively engaged in their reading to learn most effectively (Locke 1996).

The blurring between adult and children's interactive books is very evident in the toy books that were first made as novelty items in the 1820s.[9] Thomas Dean, one of the most successful publishers at the time, created the *New Scenic Books* series in the mid-1850s. These books incorporated the first pop-ups, although this term was

---

[9] University of North Texas Libraries has an extensive collection of pop-ups which can be seen at http://www.library.unt.edu/rarebooks/exhibits/popup2/introduction.htm.

not employed until much later. Each book included at least three scenes that a reader could view as a three-dimensional stage set. Another series, *Home Pantomime Toy Books*, incorporated different sized pages that, when a reader turned them, revealed changes in the scene. Figure 2.9 shows the popular fairy tale *The Beauty and the Beast* set on a proscenium stage.

Fig. 2.9 *Beauty and the Beast*. Home Pantomime Toy Books. London: Dean & Son. Circa 1873[*]

Emerging Story

In the examples provided to this point in the history of interactive narratives, the reader co-created an existing story. At that point in the development of print narrative the reader's collaboration in co-creation took on a different note. In the following examples readers are provided the opportunity to add their own intentions to the story and actively change the meaning of the story. The distinction comes from the emergent nature of narrative opportunities offered by a particular type of physical artifact.

As one of their ventures in the 1860s Dean & Son also began publishing pull-tab books in which characters were attached to pull tabs that a reader could manipulate. In the harlequinades readers would unfold and reveal parts of the story, changing the sequence but not the story. In *The Royal Punch and Judy* (see Fig. 2.10) the reader could physically manipulate the characters to act out the scenes in the story by moving pull-tabs. Although there is a traditional and very limited set of actions associated with the story, readers could, nevertheless, choose to use these actions when they felt the actions best expressed the personality of the characters and their part in the story. This was, in small measure, emergence in the process of storytelling, during which the reader collaborated with the author's story content to produce an unscripted version of the story.

---

[*]The moveable page can be seen at the UNT site: http://www.library.unt.edu/rarebooks/exhibits/popup2/dean.htm.

Fig. 2.10 *Moveable Book of the Royal Punch & Judy as Played before the Queen at Windsor Castle & the Crystal Palace.* London: Dean & Son. Circa 1861

The opportunities for the reader to collaborate with the making of the story jumped to a new level when paper dolls were included as an insert in a book. Paper dolls were introduced as play objects as early as the 1790s. Samuel and Joseph Fuller introduced paper dolls as an accessory to their stories in 1810. When they did so, they moved the engagement readers enjoyed with the story off the page into the reader's physical space and under the reader's authorial control.

The Fullers sold the first of their *Paper Figure Adventures* in their London shop *The Temple of Fancy.* In *The History and Adventures of Little Henry* (1810) readers could follow Little Henry on his adventures in a life that had him improve his status from ragamuffin to sea captain. Unlike other paper dolls which consisted of a base doll with clothes that could be put on and taken off the figure, these early cut outs consisted of sets of clothes in stand-up scenes with the character's head as a separate object that could be moved from one set up to another. The author provided a text for readers to follow and Henry's set ups suggested how the character should be played in a particular scene. Readers could follow the sequence of the written narrative or could act out scenes in a different sequence. Once they had Henry physically in their hands they could also take complete authorial control and add new plot twists or make up completely new stories about him. That same year the Fullers also published Little Fanny with her own set of adventures (Fig. 2.11).

Both pull-tab characters and paper dolls offered readers more than a collaboration with the author's text to co-construct an existing story, they offered agency through a simple affordance: tangible characters that could be controlled to construct an emerging rather than static narrative.

Fig. 2.11 *The History and Adventures of Little Fanny, exemplified in a series of Figures.* A. and J. Fuller, London, 1810

Production Teams

Underlying the narrative experience was the production team that collaborated to create the narrative artifact. In the eighteenth and nineteenth century, not only print narratives but performance narratives: plays, puppet theatres, opera, and ballet, provided opportunities for authors, artists, musicians, and producers to work together to collaboratively create, develop, and bring stories to an audience. In some cases the scripts/texts were the responsibility of one writer, such as the libretto for Mozart's opera *Figaro*, written by Lorenzo da Ponte. In other cases texts were the result of authors working collaboratively in teams. George Melchiori tells us in his introduction to Shakespeare's *King Edward III* that after 1597 records of receipts for payment to playwrights "were to teams of three or more working on single plays, or to add writers for 'additions' to existing play-books. There could be no better evidence that play-writing for public playhouses was originally conceived as a collective endeavor, in which no doubt the actors themselves had the last word" (Shakespeare 1998, p. 13).[10]

Collaborating in teams on narrative was exemplified in the twentieth century by the production team required for movies. Early movies "began as novelty not as narrative." Scenes were produced from written synopsis, sometimes as short as one-line descriptions. Without sound, film scenes could be obscure and viewers needed cues to follow. The synopsis, which, like the title cards, provided continuity, was

---

[10] Production teams that include authors working collaboratively with other specialists go back significantly farther then the sixteenth century, at least to ancient Greek theatre and probably to Ancient Egyptian narratives. The topic is unfortunately not the pervue of this book.

often printed to hand out to viewers both as promotional material and to help them understand the film.[11] During this early period it was also common for a lecturer or bonimenteur to explain the film to viewers. The delivery and reception of early films was an exercise in improvised collaboration: necessity dictated.

When films became longer after 1900 the requirements for a cohesive narrative became greater and so did the need for scripts. The first scripts were lists of scenes that identified what was to be in the picture. It was up to the director to work collaboratively with his production team so that scenes unfolded cohesively in front of the camera. One of the first movies for which an extensive scenario list was made was Georges Melies's *Trip to the Moon* (*Le voyage dans la lune, 1902*). By 1915, however, movie scripts had become "not merely scripts but, in fact, complex packages comprised of multiple production documents" (Gay 2011). Informal and improvised collaborative teams were soon of a standard comparable to those of major newspapers or publishing houses.[12] For the audience, who at one time had engaged with the film via title cards, a lecturer, musicians, and a printed synopsis card, co-creation of the film became more cognitive and less tangible as these forms merged into the talking films of today.

Of all the performance narratives, one was noted for offering interactive opportunities for the audience. British pantomimes (Pantos) were based in the Italian Commedia dell'arte as translated by the British Music Hall tradition. Introduced by actor manager John Rich in 1717 (Theatre Britain 2015) the first performances encouraged collaboration between the actors and the audience in the form of verbal exchanges intended to engage the audience in moving the performance forward. This tradition has continued until today with the production of contemporary pantos (all based on traditional stories) in which the patter between the actors and the audience is expected and formulaic. The audience is asked to cheer the hero/heroine, boo the victim, and to participate in a dialogue exchange with the characters. The audience, familiar with the patter, willingly and enthusiastically collaborates with the actors in turning in a performance. *A Short History of British Pantomime* (2010) share the following dialogue:

> Ugly sister: "I'm much prettier than Cinderella"
> Audience: "Oh no you're not!"
> Ugly sister: "Oh yes I am!"
> Audience: "Oh no you're not!"

---

[11] The synopsis for *Pillow Fight,* an 1897 film made by Edison Studios, read "Four young ladies, in their nightgowns, are having a romp. One of the pillows gets torn, and the feathers fly all over the room." More examples at http://www.screenplayology.com/content-sections/screenplay-style-use/1-1.

[12] Telephone, radio, and television narratives were similarly produced by a team of authors and directors working collaboratively to create a narrative artifact.

Choose Your Own Adventure

A major innovation in how authors and readers collaborated in narrative print environments came about in 1979 with the *Choose Your Own Adventure* (CYOA) series of books. CYOA were game books in which the reader determined the main characters' actions and the plot's outcome. While text adventure games were already a reality in the computer world at that time—Will Crowther had created *Adventure* in 1975—computers and game consoles were yet to become a common household presence and the audience for these early games was very limited; print was still sovereign.

The CYOA series originated as a bedtime story that the author Edward Packard was telling his two daughters one evening. When he asked them what happened next, they each gave a different answer. Packard provided an ending for both ideas and the branching story evolved from there. He produced a manuscript of the story with all of its branches but wasn't very successful with selling it and put it aside until he saw an ad placed by a small publisher looking for innovative books. Interested in his concept of an interactive book in which the audience played a part in choosing an outcome, Vermont Crossroads Press accepted and published the manuscript as *The Adventures of You on Sugarcane Island* in 1976 (Hendrix 2011). The company subsequently sold the rights to much larger Bantam Press who were excited about the idea of interactive books and wanted to launch a series entitled *Choose Your Own Adventure*. Packard wrote the first book, *The Cave of Time*, in the new series.

The Cave of Time was 118 pages long and had forty different endings (Lodge 2007). Figure 2.12 shows the cover art promoting "You're the star of the story! Choose from 40 possible endings" and the narrative map for the story. It was difficult to strike a right balance between interactivity and narrative in print books. To have 30 or 40 endings in a book that was less than 150 pages meant only 6 or 7 pages for each scenario. As pointed out by one of the authors, Raymond Montgomery, that number of pages didn't allow for much character, setting, or plot development. The number of endings grew fewer as the series progressed, until in the final books there were as few as ten endings with more narrative complexity in each scenario—interactivity gave way to narrative in print (Neilsen 2002).

Between 1979–1998, 180 different CYOA books were produced and 250 million copies of these were sold. The enthusiasm for the books shows that readers had a high level of interest in engaging interactively with a story in which they were given the agency to directly affect how the story developed and ended. The interest in interactivity in storytelling exhibited by these avid audiences was readily embraced and vigorously actualized in the emerging world of digital narrative games. Although the readers might have been common to both, it would be difficult to ascertain whether CYOA was a direct influence on early text adventure games. At least in one case, it wasn't. Shortly after he'd

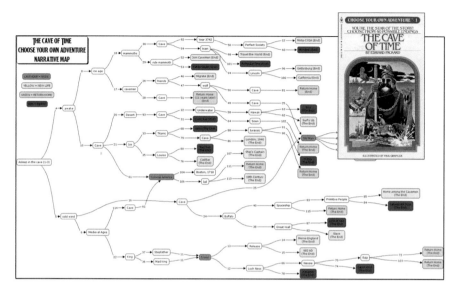

Fig. 2.12 *The Cave of Time*, 1979, cover and narrative map[*]

created the text adventure game *Zork* in 1977, David Lebling saw the *Choose Your Own Adventure Series* and thought it was a knock-off—someone was "trying to do an adventure game as a book" which had a lot less interactivity then a text game (Hendrix 2011).[13]

The next section provides an introduction into the history of the symbiotic rise of interactive fiction and the technologies of new media and the approach taken to accommodate interest in being a participating partner in story evolution.

---

[*]The narrative map of *The Cave of Time* can be found at http://www.samplereality.com/gmu/fall2008/343/wp-content/uploads/2008/09/caveoftime.jpg. A structural analysis is at: http://samizdat.cc/cyoa/gallery/cave-of-time.html.

[13]Interactivity in books would take a different turn as publishers began to explore the more extensive use of photos and manipulables. An example of a successful contemporary interactive book is *The* Bob Dylan *Scrapbook*. This biography consists of text, images, an audio CD of interviews, removable facsimilies such as handwritten song lyrics, and pull-up flaps. Simon & Schuster. New York, NY. 2005.

Chapter 3
Narrative as Material Practice: A Digital Domain

Hypertext, hypermedia, and interactive fiction are genres of narrative based in digital delivery methods that result from an evolving dance between authors and computer scientists, between narrative and technology. In *Hamlet on the Holodeck* Janet Murray eloquently foretold a future for digital narrative that was expansive and participatory and that reflected its symbiotic and interdependent nature.

> *I find myself anticipating a new kind of storyteller, one who is half hacker, half bard … I see glimmers of a medium that is capacious and broadly expressive … [that] promise[s] to reshape the spectrum of narrative expression, not by replacing the novel or the movie but by continuing their timeless bardic work within another framework … . [Hamlet on the Holodeck] is an attempt to imagine a future digital medium, shaped by the hacker's spirit and the enduring power of the imagination … . (Murray 1997, pp. 9–10)*

Murray presented four affordances of digital media: that it was procedural, encyclopedic, spatial, and participatory. The participatory nature of digital media was defined by the interactivity it affords for dialogue and collaboration.

Hypertext: Connecting Information

Hypertext has played a major role in changing our concepts of dialogue and collaboration for authors and readers of narratives. Computer technology offered a new model for narrative when it introduced linking as a way to connect information. In her 1988 article, *A Grand Vision*, Janet Fiderio wrote:

© The Author(s) 2016
K. Madej, *Interactivity, Collaboration, and Authoring in Social Media*,
International Series on Computer Entertainment and Media Technology,
DOI 10.1007/978-3-319-25952-9_3

Hypertext, at its most basic level, is a DBMS [data base management system] that lets you connect screens of information using associative links. At its most sophisticated level, hypertext is a software environment for collaborative work, communication, and knowledge acquisition. (Fiderio 1988)

Computer-based hypertext was conceived by Ted Nelson while he was devising a "text-handling system which would allow writers to revise, compare, and undo their work easily" as a graduate student at Harvard in the early 1960s (Moulthrop 2002). In 1965, Nelson worked with Dr. Andries van Dam and his students at Brown University to develop one of the very first hypertext-based systems, HES (Hypertext Editing System).[1] The term hypertext described "the use of computers to express the nonlinear structure of written ideas" (Bonime and Pohlmann 1998, p. 45) and encompassed the notion that it could convey the interconnectedness and complexity of knowledge (Keep 1993). At that time van Dam had a difficult time convincing the vice-president of the university that their programs should be allowed on the university research computers. According to the VP, "If it [text program] was there, people would use it which would subvert the real purpose of computing: to produce numbers not words" (Neilson). Originally, IBM, the sponsor for their research couldn't be told that their expensive graphics terminals were being used "just for displaying words" (Neilson). In 1967 van Dam and his research team developed a second, more advanced, hypertext system, FRESS (The File Retrieval and Editing SyStem) that pioneered among other things, the Undo command, and was so successful a version was still running on Brown's mainframe in 1999 (DeRose). Through the 1960s electronic text document delivery became an important issue for "high-tech industries (because their technical documentation is so huge), and humanities scholars (because their document processing is sophisticated)" (DeRose). An example of the very early use to which hypertext and electronic text was put is Project Gutenberg, a storage and retrieval system of books in the public domain. There are now over 49,000 Project Gutenberg eTexts available. Volunteers collaborate through a Distributed Proofreaders team to add texts.[2]

---

[1] Nelson had been looking for a text handling system that would more closely resemble the free association of human thought process rather than the linear process of printed text (1960).

[2] In 1971, the operators of XEROX Sigma V mainframe (Michael's best friend and his brothers best friend) at the University of Illinois gave Michael Hart, then a student at the university, a $100,000,000 computer time operator's account and encouraged him to do whatever he wanted (in the spirit of "he might find something exciting and new to do"). Hart felt there wasn't anything he could do in the way of normal computing that would create that value. "An hour and 47 min later, he announced that the greatest value created by computers would not be computing, but would be the storage, retrieval, and searching of what was stored in our libraries." Project Gutenberg was born. The project's philosophy became to make texts available to the general public in the easiest-to-use-form for the broadest possible dissemination. Project eTexts (or electronic texts) were created in "Plain Vanilla ASCII because "99% of the hardware and software a person is likely to run into can read and search these files" (Hart, The History and Philosophy of Project Gutenberg 1992).

During the same period Doug Engelbart was working with his team at the Augmentation Research Center to create a "hyper collaborative knowledge environment system called NLS" (Englebart 2008). Engelbert was interested in giving users powerful tools for collaborating in the computer environment. In 1968 Engelbart demonstrated the completed system at the Fall Joint Computer Conference in San Francisco. The ground-breaking computer features included: windows, hypertext, graphics, video conferencing, the computer mouse, word processing, dynamic file linking, revision control and a collaborative real-time editor. These features increased individual's ability to manipulate text and image, to communicate them both locally and remotely, and to dialogue and work collaboratively over distance. Astonishing to those at the conference, which later became known as *The Mother of All Demos*, was not only the comprehensive and visionary approach and the practical results achieved by Englebart's team but also the leading-edge technologies used in the presentation. Engelbart demonstrated hypertext and collaborative editing on his onstage terminal, shown on a 22 ft. screen, as members of his team (working 30 miles away) were teleconferenced in via telephone lines. Figure 3.1a. shows an image of Engelbart operating NLS superimposed on an image of the overhead screen during the presentation. Figure 3.1b. shows a demo of the NLS teleconferencing system featuring one of the team members from Memlo Park.

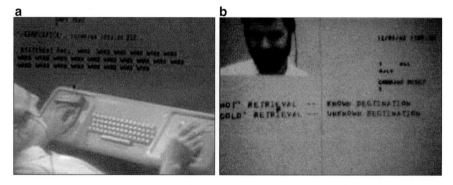

Fig. 3.1 *The Mother of All Demos.* (**a**) Image of Engelbart operating NLS superimposed on image of the overhead screen. (**b**) Demonstration of the teleconferencing system showing one of the team members from Memlo Park

The presentation successfully demonstrated the collaborative nature of computer technologies and their effectiveness in bringing people together to engage in knowledge work on both a small and large scale. Many of the features presented would influence the subsequent development of hypermedia tools.

Labyrinth

In September 1970, *Software*, an important and influential exhibit offered new perspectives on the dialogue between technology and art. It was presented at the Jewish Museum in New York and was subsequently shown at the Smithsonian Institution in December of that year. Rather than looking at how technologies could be or were being used for artistic purposes, the intent of the exhibition was to look at the rapidly growing information processing systems and how, in the future, they might redefine cultural awareness of aesthetics. Visitors to the exhibit were invited to operate computers to experience for themselves the possibilities of the technology. For the exhibit Ted Nelson created an interactive catalogue titled *Labyrinth* that was the first large-scale public use of a hypertext system. Visitors were able to consult computer stations located throughout the exhibit where they could access artist files, move to the next text, go back to the beginning of the catalogue, or access related texts, all in a non-linear fashion. There was a printing station at the end of the exhibit where those interested could get a personalized printout of the texts in the catalogue they had accessed throughout the exhibit. The catalogue became a project within a project, where the technology and the art combined in a creative framework that had been specifically designed to accommodate and reflect the content (Nelson and Woodman 1970; Bonin 2004; Rossi 2013). The computer was not presented as a single use device, i.e. a box that crunched numbers, rather it was adapted to address several contexts: accessing the catalogue and then diarizing and publishing the visit.

Labyrinth enabled readers to collaborate with the program and create individual narratives that chronicled their path through the *Software* exhibition. It was an adventurous approach to creating a personal narrative of an event as none of the process was scripted: the exhibit goer was given agency as author, the exhibit acted as content, and the hypertext system was the medium that encouraged collaboration between user and text and delivered the final narrative artifact.

Invisible Seattle[3]

> *"Now the excitement begins," the voice invites, "We have a room full of computers, printers, copiers, CRTs, pens, pencils, and billboards. Join us in writing the first computer-compiled novel written by Seattle about Seattle. Yes, written by you and your friends. Step inside and take a look. You are on your way to becoming a great author." (Waldrop 1984)*

---

[3] The *Invisible Seattle Literary Computer Project* is described and documented in Rob Wittig's Book *Invisible Rendevous* (Wittig 1994). A video is available on Wittig's site http://robwit. net/?project=invisible-seattle-the-novel-of-seattle-by-seattle.

The new ease with which data could be shared, accessed, and manipulated encouraged communities who were authoring stories collectively and collaboratively to experiment and embrace computers in their process.[4] In 1983, the writing collective *Invisible Seattle*[5] organized an extensive and multifaceted data collection and publishing event at the Bumbershoot Art Festival. Started in 1979 by Jean Sherrard, Larry Stone, James Winchell, and Philip Wohlstetter, the intent of the collective was to use words and images to change the way in which people experienced their environment.

> *Since 1979 Invisible Seattle has conspired to "take over the city by hypnotic suggestion." Each of our acts has been an attempt to inject an element of "fiction" into the so-called "reality" of an unsuspecting average American metropolis and self-proclaimed livable city. (Wittig 1994, p. 31)*

The collective's main project was the *Map of Invisible Seattle*, a complex historical, cultural, and architectural representation of the city that reflected the many visual and verbal ways, other than text, that writers could use to tell their stories. For the 1981 Bumbershoot Arts Festival the collective had staged a mock trial of the novelist Tom Robbins. The next year they held a city council meeting. "After 3 years of events," Wittig tells us in *Invisible Rendevous*, "the invisibles were ready to combine geographic investigation, the search for new forms of writing, and collaboration in an ambitious new project" (p. 48).

For the 1983 festival a group of about ten members spearheaded by Philip Wohlstetter and Rob Wittig planned and organized the collective's first literary product, *Invisible Seattle Literary Computer Project*. Conceiving the project as a public authoring event, they intended to use the city—its people and its places—as product, that is the content of the novel, and also as process, the means by which the novel was composed. Figure 3.2 shows the fill-in-the-blank announcement/invitation created for the *Literary Computer Project*. It embraces a participatory act as a condition of the event and states visually and textually the collaboration at the core of the Novel's composition.

---

[4] These are two distinctly different efforts. When people collaborate they share knowledge and work together towards a common goal. When people work collectively they each contribute their own individual effort to the work. During collaboration individuals must listen, discuss, negotiate, compromise, and problem solve.

[5] The *Invisible Seattle* collective name referenced Italo Calvino's book *Invisible Cities* and signaled the group's intent to use the city as their creative inspiration and environment for engagement.

Fig. 3.2 Fill-in-the-blank invitation to the citizens of Seattle to participate in the *Invisible Seattle Literary Computer Project*

The Literary Workers, wearing white work overalls stenciled with words, and hardhats that featured question marks, used a lighthearted, if constructivist, approach in engaging with the public, suggesting they could participate in constructing a novel, much as one would participate in constructing a building, "block by block, word by word" (Waldrop 1984). Instructed to "find the words, humor and touching anecdotes that would fill the novel" (Waldrop 1984) workers used interviews, questionnaires, and fill-in-the-blank forms to engage citizens and gather texts that represented authentic voices of the city. Workers also collected overheard conversations, favorite lies for the *Book of Lies*, songs, anecdotes, and locations for action. The data *was* the city: it would be used to publicly compose a book during the festival. Figure 3.3 shows the identity card Literary Workers used when introducing themselves to the people of Seattle and a number of the interview sessions.

The data gathering resulted in texts of different kinds (Fig. 3.4) that were collected in available boxes, bags, and binders and brought to, once it was built, an authoring venue on the Bumbershoot festival grounds. Intended to facilitate collaboration, the space included data-gathering pods made from old video game machines, clues in bubble-topped display units, bulletin boards for posting data, and a "Literary Computer," Sheherezade II, that held the technology which would facilitate the process of authoring: two micro-computers, modems, and printers. Figure 3.5 shows the venue with the clue displays leading up to Sheherezade II.

Fig. 3.3 Literary Workers engaged the citizens of Seattle to create a novel about their city through interviews, questionnaires, and fill-in-the-blank forms

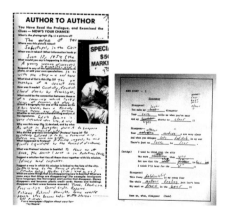

Fig. 3.4 Two kinds of data artifacts collected by Literary Workers

The writing that went on during the 4 days allocated to the novel's composition was "a hybrid of algorithmic thinking and eighteenth century technologies" (Wittig, p. 74). Computer consultant Ted Holtzman had been invited to design a system that compiled and sorted the data and would be used for text editing the novel. The actual composition of the novel was facilitated within Sheherezade II, which had been designed by collective member and sculptor Clair Colquitt to represent the co-existence of analog and digital efforts:

> ... monitors, video screens on the sides, bookshelves on the ends, and a popcorn popper on top. The cabin was large enough to contain three or four Literary Workers at a time, who were visible to the public through the small hatches. What the architecture presented to the visitors was a 3-D diagram of an algorithmic way of thinking. (Harris 1995)

Fig. 3.5 Display units with bubble shaped tops displayed clues and led visitors up to Sheherezade II

Using the two microcomputers set up in Sheherezade II, participating writers, working in pairs, were given about 2 hours to create their first draft of a chapter of the mystery from the thousands of pieces of handwritten data that had been collected and organized by the Literary Workers (Fig. 3.6). The novel was planned to have 15 chapters of eight pages each. One writer would access data and the other use the text editing program to write the text. *Guest Writers Guidelines* were put up on the wall above the computers to provide instructions (Wittig 1994) and each new pair of writers was given help for continuity in their chapter: the framework for the plot, what characters should appear from previous chapters, and photos or clues that needed to be mentioned in the chapter. The information provided included a map that showed the movement of the characters as well as local information that could be useful in developing the story: maps of the area, local histories, photos, bus schedules, etc.

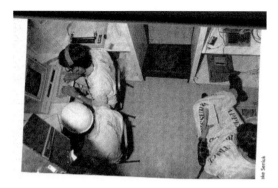

Fig. 3.6 Inside Sheherezade II, Literary Workers input data to create drafts that would be posted for the public to read and edit

Exhibit visitors were encouraged to participate and an eight track tape gave simple instructions on how to use the equipment; a few visitors did participate, however, most of the novel was written by members from the collective or by guest writers. Visitors participated more extensively by reading and making comments on the data and new drafts that were regularly posted on the walls of the venue (Fig. 3.7). These comments would be brought to the writers in Sheherezade II for consideration and inclusion in the next draft (Waldrop 1984).

Fig. 3.7 Seattle citizens participated in authoring at the event by commenting on data posted on the walls and providing feedback to drafts as they were posted

The 4 days of writing were "an exhilarating madhouse" (Wittig 1994, p. 76) that had writers searching for details in piles of data, lights flashing to announce major new ideas, and visitors laughing and commenting on drafts as newly completed chapters were printed out and posted. A draft of the complete Novel was finished at the end of 4 days. It would be a mistake, however, to think that this "madhouse" implied an unstructured visionary approach to the composition of the novel. The madhouse was governed by algorithmic planning. Figure 3.8 shows a diagram of the components of the project the collective had devised early in the history of the project.

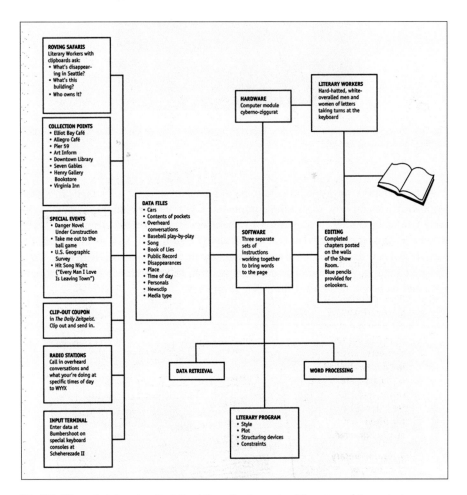

Fig. 3.8 The underlying plan disciplined the collective and public nature of the project

Those who participated in the literary event from the beginning experienced a new kind of writing that was more than they expected it to be:

> *A new image of the process of writing had replaced the Romantic one in their minds—an image of a room full of people creating within a frame of rules, reaching into big cardboard boxes for handfuls of text as needed, giving away ideas, reading fragments aloud, delighting in the prose of others, trying chunks of text in variant orders, editing in teams, writing in public for all to see.* (Wittig 1994, p. 76)

The process had shown the potential of authoring by more than one writer, and of writing that did not necessarily require completion. As a collective effort the project had collected different types of data from the people of Seattle: questionnaire forms, mad-lib style fill-in-the-blanks, clip-out-and-return coupons that encouraged including photos, overheard conversations, favorite lies for the *Book of Lies*, fill-in-the-blank words for songs (Rettberg 2005; Waldrop 1984). As a collaborative effort the collective had first collaborated on the planning and organizing of the event and then included the people of Seattle in the composition of the final novel. At the event writers (many) had worked with the texts, with each other, and with the visitors at the event to negotiate character descriptions, settings, and plot points. Individual viewpoints were invited, considered, accommodated, or not, as the Novel, the common goal, required. Working collectively and collaboratively on such a large scale introduced a new nature or essence to authoring. It revealed quite explicitly that what ended up in the novel was determined both by the data made available and by the choices exercised in assembling the data: algorithmic possibilities in which computer technology could excel and in which collaboration played a fundamental role.

The collective came to realize that the end result was not only a Novel but an opportunity—a database that was the heart, mind, and experience of Seattle which could be mined to create multiple works. This final draft was only one of many possibilities and the beginning of a long process of collaborative editing by the collective that ended in 1987 with the printing of *Invisible Seattle Version 7.1*.[6]

Hypertext Stories

The hypertext breakthrough in computer technology moved beyond special interest groups and reached the general public when affordable and user-friendly personal computers became available in the late 1970s and early 1980s. Until then, exploration of interactivity and collaborative authoring in narrative was the purview of researchers, academics, game developers, and early experimenters who wanted to explore new ways of authoring. When in 1981 Commodore introduced the VIC-20 home computer and IBM introduced its PC with MS-DOS basic software, the public was very receptive. The swiftness with which personal computers became a part of society is demonstrated by Drexel University's (Philadelphia) announcement in 1982 that it would require all students to own a personal computer. The introduction of WordPerfect in 1982 and Microsoft Word in 1983 for the PC made these first computers ideal for word processing by anyone and of particular use to writers. Apple computer had rolled out its first personal computer with a graphical user interface (GUI), Lisa, in 1983. Too expensive and too slow, it was soon replaced

---

[6]Twenty-nine years after the event, the *Invisibles* and *Invisible Seattle: the Novel of Seattle* were featured in the exhibit *Electronic Literature* at the 2012 Modern Language Association (MLA) convention in Seattle.

(winter 1984) with the Macintosh. The graphic user interface brought control of image and format as well as text. The popularization of such technology, not only in progressive university settings but with a larger general public, gave writers new audiences for their stories and new ways to tell those stories.

With the 1984 Apple introduction of the Macintosh with GUI and the Hewlett-Packard introduction of the LaserJet laser printer, authors had more control for how they created their work, modified it, shared it, stored it, and even produced it as print. Authors interested in pushing the restrictions of the page were, however, still frustrated: navigating technology to create hypertext narrative was complex and time consuming, and not a part of most author's literacy set. In 1984 author Michael Joyce met computer scientist Jay Bolter at the Yale Artificial Intelligence lab and they started work on a hypertext program that, rather than following a linear sequence as did a word processing program, would navigate text spatially. "Hypertext shows how programming and conventional prose writing can come together in the space provided by the computer, by putting at the disposal of writers data structures that programmers have used for decades" (Bolter 2001, p. 38).

Together, they created the hypertext editing system Storyspace that gave authors an environment for writing "as a flood of thoughts" (Bolter 2001, p. 33). By providing a variety of maps and views to help writers create, organize, and revise—items could be selected, moved, cut, and copied freely—Storyspace gave authors an easy transition into a technology that would help them adapt their work to different forms of representation. Hypertext could interpret networks of ideas, cross-reference them, and present them in all their complexity. The program provided access to tools for creating interactive stories in which readers could connect tangibly with ideas and construct a personally directed narrative through a collaborative process and allowed the reader to be an active rather than a passive participant in a dynamic narrative space. Ultimately "hypertext alters writing … by increasing the power of expression and challenging the inventive process of both authors and … readers" (Hawkes 1998, p. 19).

An early example of interactive hypertext fiction is *afternoon*, written by Michael Joyce in 1986 and published by Eastgate Systems as their first hypertext. Written using Storyspace, the story is a literary fiction in which readers weave their way along paths they choose through a network of textual spaces: all paths are equal and no single path is dominant. The author has structured the network so the links create relationships the readers can follow to experience a story rather than chaos (Bolter 2001). The collaboration here is between reader and the programmed text, with the story creation based in information written and networked by the author, Joyce. While there are many choices for moving through the hypertext, in spirit, the interactivity is similar to that in the print *Choose Your Own Adventure* stories.

Stuart Moulthrop's *Victory Garden* (1995) added considerable complexity to the paths a reader could take through a story and continued to move the emerging genre of interactive fiction forward. Creating a network of 990 episodes and 2800, or so, links, Moulthrop encouraged readers to collaboratively compose their own story(ies) about the fictitious character Emily Runbird and activities she was involved in during the Gulf War. On first entry, the reader was offered a series of choices for ways to navigate the story: the map of the garden, the lists of paths, or the composition of a sentence. The reader's journey provided views of the characters from different viewpoints depending on the path and the individual parts of the path chosen. Figure 3.9 shows the sampler page from Eastgate, the publisher, with four entry choices. In this sampler the reader can navigate through 105 spaces and is offered 500 links to reach these spaces in different configurations.

The difference for a reader between the hypertext *Victory Garden* and the print *Choose Your Own Adventure* was more than quantitative. The conventions of the printed book that restricted readers to text on a page lost their power in an electronic environment. In this case quantity did equal quality as the opportunity for more extensive linking added depth to characters and settings and gave readers the opportunity to become more intricately involved in the story. The tangible participation of making decisions to generate a personally directed path through the narrative provided a strong sense of collaborating in creating the story.

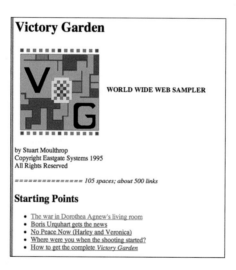

Fig. 3.9 *Victory Garden* Sampler provided four starting points into the story

Hypertexts carried on the tradition of reader manipulation of texts offered by interactive narratives such as lift-the-flap harlequinades and *Choose Your Own Adventure* books. The quantity of texts (lexia) and the multiple ways in which texts could be combined to create the final narrative in hypertext (and then hypermedia) environments created a narrative experience that inhabited a much larger narrative space than did experiences with earlier and simpler narrative artifacts. Virtual worlds were being created in which author's texts and reader's choices co-habited and defined paths to the author's endings.

In 1987 Apple introduced Hypercard, an easy to use programming tool which provided Amanda Goodenough the means to create the first graphical hypertext, *Inigo Gets Out*.[7] HyperCard was offered free with all Macintosh computers and

---

[7] Produced by The Voyageur Company. View currently (July 2015) at https://www.youtube.com/watch?v=MxN8ZlIAwsI.

made the use of hypermedia a fact rather than a theory for authors who weren't tech savvy as they could finally take advantage of interactivity and multimodality in constructing their narratives. Goodenough's motivation to create interactive stories was her experience of storytelling with her grandmother. During their story time together her grandmother's constant question "what do you think happens next?" was an instigation to create new storylines. Goodenough was encouraged to reflect on her own reality and shaped her interpretation of the story accordingly. When she took control of the story and moved it in the direction she wanted to, she became the author. Goodenough found HyperCard could be used to create the interactive environment in which children could participate to create a story. She chose the application because it "was so easy to use that I was able to create a simple interactive story" (Goodenough).[8] With the ability to manipulate image and format as well as text, the author could offer readers a larger landscape in which to interact with stories. This became more desirable as affordable computers entered the market and increased the audience for interactive and collaborative stories.

Interaction is de facto in hypertext and hypermedia. In the hypertext *Marble Springs* (1993), reader's participation in collaborating on the story is also solicited. In the novel, also created in HyperCard, author Deena Larsen describes a town and a set of fully realized characters. Readers can choose a path to follow from a network of storylines. Larson then adds to this network a new level of interactivity. She asks readers to send her their own ideas for the story and participate in its ongoing creation. She has sketched out a number of characters and invites the reader to complete them.

> SEND YOUR WRITING of any kind (prose, poetry, or researched articles; on paper, computer disk, or a modified copy of Marble Springs with a list of all changes) to be considered for the new edition of Marble Springs (1997 publication). Or call or e-mail with any questions. All authors and their contributions will be credited.[9]

In adding a request for reader submissions and then including the submissions to the narrative, Larson has changed the tenor of the collaboration from one of recombining information to create story to one of emergence and creation of a new story. There is, however, a proviso. The reader is not directly in charge of the emerging narrative, in fact, the reader's suggestion may not be used at all. The reader has a potential to become a collaborating author, but only at the behest of the main author, and even then, where or how the suggestion is used is not in their control. It appears that authorial agency has been given to the reader; in fact, the reader has less authorial agency than in the nineteenth century pull-up *The Royal Punch and Judy*, in which readers physically manipulated the characters of the play when they chose to do so.

---

[8] Goodenough met Bob Stein, founder of the multimedia publishing company Voyager, at a MacWorld Expo software exchange meeting. Goodenough recounts: "I said bravely, 'This is *Inigo Gets Out.*' He immediately said, 'You must be Amanda Goodenough. I'm Bob Stein of the Voyager Company. I want to publish your work.' Talk about dreams coming true!" (Goodenough 2007). Stein also subsequently published *Amanda Stories*. He is the founder of the Institute for the Future of the Book at http://www.futureofthebook.org.

[9] 1993 version at http://www.eastgate.com/MS/Title_184.html. 2014 version at http://marblesprings.wikidot.com.

Hypermedia

In 1978, Andrew Lippman developed the landmark *Aspen Movie Map*, the "first true hypermedia system." Working at the time with the MIT Architecture Machine Group, Lippman took a team of researchers to Aspen, Colorado where they moved through the streets of Aspen and used four different cameras to take photos at intervals of the street scenes. They linked these photos in four directions: back, forward, left, and right, and provided a navigation map, so that not only could the user move in any of the directions at any time, he could also start at any point on a virtual tour of the town (Abrams). The freedom of movement in any and every direction that was the signature of hypertext was brought to video and added to the hypermedia mix available for author's use.

One of the first complex and ambitious hypermedia works was the novel *Califia* started by M.D. Coverley (Marjorie Coverley Luesebrink) in 1995 and published by Eastgate Systems in 2000. Coverley/Luesebrink, an educator and early adopter of digital technologies in literature, commented about emerging digital literary forms at a conference in 2002: "Basically, there have been two approaches to encouraging readers to become involved with electronic literature. The first is to insist that electronic narrative is just like print narrative—look, we can print it out! The other, more risky route, is to venture that electronic literature is evolving into a new form of storytelling prose—still literature, still narrative, but with its own characteristic. Because the work that interests me most really can not be printed out, I tend to see hypertext narratives as moving toward a new form of literature" (Luesebrink).

M.D. Coverley created her story as a mix of text, image, graphics, video, and sound—before the technology to add all of these elements to her text was readily available. Knowledge of the technology and what it can do, and being able to manipulate it, affects how the narrative develops. She has said, "I see the story complete with pictures and sound in my head. The question is whether I can manipulate the technology to represent what I think" (Luesebrink). In *Hamlet on the Holodeck* Janet Murray comments "By giving us greater control over different kinds of information, [computers] invite us to tackle more complex tasks and to ask new kinds of questions" (Murray). Working at the vanguard of hypermedia literature, Coverley was dealing with new questions about the use of multiple modes of representation, interactivity, and collaboration in storytelling.

Over 5 years following the start of work on the novel in 1995 Coverley explored and took advantage of evolving technology as it became available. She expanded *Califia* into a complex landscape of networked lexias and refashioned the novel genre to make it into a multimedia experience. In *Califia* Coverley brought readers a story about five generations of Californians on a quest to find a lost treasure of gold.[10] She created a virtual space, a hypermedia world of visual and textual artifacts, that represented both fictional and real characters, history, geology, maps, and legends that were related to the quest she set (Leusebrink 2002). Readers were

---

[10] http://califia.us/califia1.htm.

invited to follow the story according to their own preferences — they could follow any one of three main characters and four principle paths through the surface events that moved the story forward. A wealth of secondary information was available to be mined by readers; when accessed, these created the density of a Victorian novel. The reader had the choice to move on the surface or to dig deeper and gain more insight into the characters and the story. Ultimately the reader arrived at an ambiguous ending: the treasure was located but would take considerable effort to unearth: the process of searching was shown as more important than the outcome, the adventure more a metaphysical quest than a conventional mystery.

The story of *Califia* is based in historical fact, and the reader was encouraged to find out more by going to the local library and bringing new knowledge to the understanding of the story. We all bring contextual information to our readings, and some readers are motivated to find out more; the directive from the author to do so invited a collaboration that was acknowledged rather than being a given. Figure 3.10a shows an introductory screen with the invitation "Come Ashore" that linked the readers to the story appearing on the screen through both a textual directive and a visual reference: an image of footprints. The invitation to participate continued when readers were asked to "Follow Me" — a suggestion to follow the footprints of an individual "Me" (Fig. 3.10b).

Fig. 3.10 Introductory frames: (**a**) *Once there was an island called California where dreams came true … Come ashore.* (**b**) *On the day after my father was buried, I began digging on the hill behind the house in Whitley Heights. The air was hot and the wind was rising. Follow Me*

The screen in Fig. 3.11a shows readers three paths they could follow through the story, Kaye's, Calvin's, and Augusta's. Figure 3.11b shows different compass points at which the readers could enter the story and shows the backstories that readers could access. Depending on their preference, readers could follow one character from the beginning to the end of the story. They might not have accessed the depth of information available when they did so, but they would have followed the major plotline. This did not negate the agency they were provided: their choice was to take the most direct path. More of the same type of choice does not make the narrative more interactive, more collaborative, or provide more agency, rather, the kind of choices that are provided, do so.

Fig. 3.11 Entry points: (**a**) Three paths: Kaye's, Calvin's, Augusta's. (**b**) Compass points: Go South I. The Comets in the yard; Go East II. Wind, Sand, and Stars; Go North III. Night of the Bear; Go West IV. The Journey Out. Back stories: Maps, Histories, Stars, and others

Coverley/Luesebrink has said about the process of producing the digital novel, "From conception to final creation, the electronic story-making process is much more time-consuming. It also requires more skills (or collaboration with others who have those talents), and extends much of the way into the 'production' that normally is assumed by a publisher" (Luesebrink). Her electronic story-making challenged existing horizons and pushed notions of narrative.

The reader was not only complicit in co-constructing the originally presented novel. As in *Marble Springs*, readers were asked to participate by sending their own experiences of the quest to the author. And as with the invitation to *Marble Springs*, authorial agency and emergence in the story because of this participation was illusory. As a collective effort, control of the story was ultimately in the hands of the originating author; the reader's experience remained that of a participant whose work was collected and might be used.

Text Adventure Antecedents: *ELIZA* and *SHRDLU*

In literary circles interactive narrative was evolving as hypermedia, in gaming interactive narrative was evolving as text adventures. In the 1960s when the first computer games emerged from the research labs of universities and computer companies they took two directions: arcade type games (*Spacewars*) and text adventures (*Adventure*). Text adventures evolved from early computer research into natural-language dialogue such as the *ELIZA*/Doctor scripts and *SHRDLU*. These programs engaged readers through question and answer formats that provided the dialogue necessary for figuring out how to fulfill the game quest and that came to embody the format of text adventures and early role playing games.

ELIZA is a program that made natural language conversation with a computer possible. Written at MIT's Artificial Intelligence Lab between 1964 and 1966 by Joseph Weizenbaum, it was based on simple pattern recognition that required very little programmed information. In the program a fictional therapist responded to a series of questions from the reader/user using a mock-Rogerian psychotherapist script based in a stimulus-response model. *ELIZA*[11] introduced the use of personal pronoun transformations that create an impression of understanding and encouraged participation and dialogue: The robot responded to "I am unhappy" with "Do you think coming here will help you not to be unhappy?" (Weizenbaum 1966). Through such responses the program created an environment of inclusion and interest that encouraged the reader to continue participating. As two-way communication, a dialogue presupposes that each participant both speaks and comprehends and both participants influence the content and form of the discourse (Cyrul 2007). The *ELIZA* dialogue was an *illusion* as there was only one participant who influenced the content. The important development in *ELIZA* was that the computer could read and respond to natural language messages typed on a computer keyboard.

SHRDLU[12] was an early AI system based on a language parser that accepted information, executed commands, and answered questions through a dialogue in English. Terry Winograd, who worked on the program in 1968–1970 at MIT, believed the best way to develop complex language models was to first write a

---

[11] Talk to *ELIZA* at http://www.masswerk.at/elizabot/.

[12] The program was named after the second row of keys on a Linotype machine.

program that could understand the language in a limited domain. Winograd said, "In general, a use involving detailed knowledge of any specific subject can rely on deduction, while an application needing superficial knowledge of a wide range of subjects can benefit from association, and will be correspondingly weak in its ability to give specific responses" (Winograd 1971, p. 421). The AI programs that worked best and gave the most realistic answers were detail specific with limited parameters for movements with clearly defined contexts. In *SHRDLU* there was a robot that had a hand and an eye and could manipulate toy blocks. Users could ask the robot to move and stack blocks of different shapes and colors and create new constructions out of these blocks that they could then name. The program was important because it had four principles that helped to create a true dialogue between the user and the program and which influenced future work in digital narratives of all kinds.

1. The *SHRDLU* world was simple and could be described in around 50 simple nouns and verbs. Figure 3.12 shows the *SHRDLU* model.
2. *SHRDLU* used basic memory and built a model of its actions so it could search back to supply context. *SHRDLU* could respond to a question about how it completed a requested task in simple sentences:

   How did you do it?

   By putting a large red block on the table; then letting go of it; then putting a large green cube on it; then letting go of that cube; then putting the red cube on that cube; then letting go of that cube.

3. Because of this memory *SHRDLU* could search in its memory for what was possible and what was not. For example: It remembered if stacking a square on a triangle had not worked previously and used this knowledge to ask questions as well as for future moves.

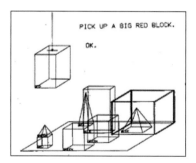

Fig. 3.12 *SHRDLU*'s structures and basic dialogue

4. *SHRDLU* remembered combinations and what they were named, and could respond to future requests for a particular construction.

These four ideas: simplicity, context, possibility, and combinations, helped actuate dialogue in later text adventures (Winograd 1971; Ward 2002).[13]

SHRDLU was not a simulation—it put into practice ideas about problem solving through understanding how natural language works. With simple English, users could configure geometric figures in any way they chose. They could give the new object a name that the program would remember. The program was able to carry a thread of conversation and provide participation without the need for predetermined paths. As users took advantage of the contextual memory of the program they were offered authorial agency that was emergent in nature. There was no scripted end. User and program worked together to create a completely new narrative. *SHRDLU* offered authorial agency through real dialogue in this small world of geometric figures that could also be effective when patterned in narrative situations.

Antecedents of the first text adventure games included interactive book series such as *The Cave of Time* and fantasy role-playing tabletop games such as *Dungeons and Dragons* that first became popular in the mid-1970s.[14] Games such as *D&D* were open-ended performance narratives that took shape when groups of players, sometimes small, sometimes large, met on a regular basis to collaborate on authoring the events of an ongoing narrative they constructed over time. Players assumed the roles of characters in a story and took part in the narrative using maps to determine location and setting and representative figurines as personal avatars. The characters could attempt various actions but were controlled by the game master who decided on the effect of a character's efforts by using personal judgment and dice, often twenty-sided, to introduce unpredictability. The meta-narrative or overarching story provided structure across all the groups, that is, they were of a specific fantasy or adventure. Building the world and moving the story forward through action, required collaboration among the players. A Dungeon Master (DM) acted as a lead storyteller and referee in each group; the details for each adventurer, the settings, and the activities in which they took part were customized within the group setting. The game was disciplined and had rules: players imagined and created action that was refereed by the DM. Players had agency as a group; in each group, each player's agency was moderated by the rules, by chance roles of the dice, and ultimately by the DM. The group participated in authorial collaboration; as was the case with agency, each player's authorial collaboration was tempered by the rules and by the DM's decisions. We look at these rules and referee decisions as similar to but not the same as the authorial control held by authors in hypertexts such as *Marble Springs* when authors invited readers to send in suggestions for creating characters or extending the narrative. In *D&D*, there existed collaboration among the group about the direction of the narrative with the DM leading as a facilitator rather than as editor.

---

[13] The dialogue used in the *SHRDLU* demo can be seen at: http://hci.stanford.edu/winograd/shrdlu/.

[14] Tabletop roleplaying games used many of the traditional narrative genres: contemporary action/adventure/espionage/military; fantasy; historical/period adventure; horror; humor and satire; science fiction; superhero; multi-genre and cross-genre.
http://en.wikipedia.org/wiki/List_of_role-playing_games_by_genre.

Adventure

Adventure is considered to be the first digital text adventure. Will Crowther, a computer programmer who had been part of the BBN team that had created ARPANET, designed the original program in 1975. Crowther and his wife Patricia, both caving/rockclimbing enthusiasts, had mapped their favorite spelunking site, the Mammoth Cave system in Kentucky, before this. In *Adventure* Crowther recreated the environment that he knew intimately and through which he could authentically guide a player. The layout in the game was a faithful reproduction of sections of the cave system and cavers who played the game could easily navigate through those familiar sections of the cave on their first visit. Crowther's text, which was simple and realistic, set the tone for the adventure, as did the puzzles, humor, combat, and fantasy he built into it. Obstacles, difficulties, and adventures included "capturing a strangely passive little bird, watching the improbable defeat of a fierce snake, conjuring up a magical crystal bridge, teleporting via magic words, and fighting with dwarves whose corpses vanish" (Jerz 2007). The game supplied the player with a lantern that ran down as the game was being played; at the point the lantern went out engagement with the story ended. One of the game's followers brought it to Stanford where Don Woods found it on a computer. Woods wanted to build on the game and he reiterated it in light of his interest in Tolkien, adding more fantasy elements as well as puzzles. At this point games were for single players; Crowther's, Wood's, and subsequent iterations employed dialogue between the player and the computer within a programmed set of actions and a defined outcome. Figure 3.13 shows an introductory screen from the program:

```
.run adven

WELCOME TO ADVENTURE!!  WOULD YOU LIKE INSTRUCTIONS?

yes

SOMEWHERE NEARBY IS COLOSSAL CAVE, WHERE OTHERS HAVE FOUND FORTUNES IN
TREASURE AND GOLD, THOUGH IT IS RUMORED THAT SOME WHO ENTER ARE NEVER
SEEN AGAIN.  MAGIC IS SAID TO WORK IN THE CAVE.  I WILL BE YOUR EYES
AND HANDS.  DIRECT ME WITH COMMANDS OF 1 OR 2 WORDS.  I SHOULD WARN
YOU THAT I LOOK AT ONLY THE FIRST FIVE LETTERS OF EACH WORD, SO YOU'LL
HAVE TO ENTER "NORTHEAST" AS "NE" TO DISTINGUISH IT FROM "NORTH".
(SHOULD YOU GET STUCK, TYPE "HELP" FOR SOME GENERAL HINTS.  FOR INFOR-
MATION ON HOW TO END YOUR ADVENTURE, ETC., TYPE "INFO".)
                              - - -
THIS PROGRAM WAS ORIGINALLY DEVELOPED BY WILLIE CROWTHER.  MOST OF THE
FEATURES OF THE CURRENT PROGRAM WERE ADDED BY DON WOODS (DON @ SU-AI).
CONTACT DON IF YOU HAVE ANY QUESTIONS, COMMENTS, ETC.

YOU ARE STANDING AT THE END OF A ROAD BEFORE A SMALL BRICK BUILDING.
AROUND YOU IS A FOREST.  A SMALL STREAM FLOWS OUT OF THE BUILDING AND
DOWN A GULLY.

east

YOU ARE INSIDE A BUILDING, A WELL HOUSE FOR A LARGE SPRING.

THERE ARE SOME KEYS ON THE GROUND HERE.

THERE IS A SHINY BRASS LAMP NEARBY.

THERE IS FOOD HERE.
```

Fig. 3.13 *Adventure* as it appeared on a PDP 10 in 1977

In addition to setting the scene, the program required input from the player that it asked for directly or implied:

> Program: Welcome to Adventure! Would you like instructions?
> Player: Yes
> Program: ... A small stream flows out the building and down the gulley.
> Player: East
> Program: You are inside a building ...

The dialogue reflected the reader and program progressing forward in tandem, each supporting the other's move towards negotiating the cave space. The program put up obstacles and challenges, the player learned through trial and error how to surmount these. Unlike today's games during which players can save their position, in early games when players were killed (as in by a dwarf) they were required to start again and replay sections they were familiar with.

Early on, not only individual programmers such as Woods adapted earlier versions of the game by extending characters, settings, and game play. User groups took it upon themselves to comment on and improve the adventure texts they played and created communities that worked collaboratively to advance the game (Jerz 2007). These user groups became a valued part of the development process for narrative and games in the digital world and also created an environment that encouraged an open-source community.

The narrative experience in *Adventure* was in the dialogue between the player and the program. The language parser that translated the player's instructions into commands could only input two word combinations such as "go west" or "drink water." The source code for the game showed the game as sets of actions that resulted from combinations of choices. The dialogue between player and program resulted in directions that were new for the player but were a part of an existing complex network of actions that had been set out by the author. Different kinds of interactive texts were reflected. A volvelle combined texts to reveal messages; the many outcomes were quite arbitrary. Harlequinades could be opened in either a specified sequence or be revealed capriciously, but their stories were short and the number of interactions very limited. Print text adventures offered readers numerous roads and different endings through a story but each path was sketchy and limited in its descriptive qualities. Each of these was limited by the media in which the content resided. As a result of residing in a media that could set aside these past limitations, the text adventure became the next step in the evolution of interactive stories. The actions of the player were not arbitrary, the interactions available were plentiful, and the situations complex. What *Adventure* did not yet do was to offer narrative emergence as the paper dolls in *The Adventures of Henry* did. *Adventure* offered opportunity to recombine existing texts to achieve an end but did not yet offer players the opportunity to create a story outside the network of text that was provided.

Zork

As a narrative *Adventure* offered players a way of interacting with different paths in the story on a more micro level than did print text adventures such as *The Cave of Time*. As noted earlier, when David Lebling first saw *The Cave of Time*, he thought it was a knock-off, that someone was "trying to do an adventure game as a book" that had a lot less interactivity than a text game (Hendrix 2011). There were print adventure scenarios that included as many as 40 endings, however, the size of the print book limited the complexity of the paths. In digital text adventures there were no such limitations. Authors could include extensive details for each setting and situation, building complex worlds to explore through multiple paths that were linked in non-linear ways. The complexity of choices created an *illusion* that players had autonomy and that their actions could alter the direction or outcome of the story, in much the same way that the hypertext *Victory Garden*, with its 990 episodes and 2800 or so links, did. The illusion of control strengthened as the technology improved and players could participate in authoring through descriptive dialogue rather than with simple two-word directives (from *Adventure* to *Zork*—see below), but the nature of the control did not change with the added complexity.

Zork, the most notable of the generation of text adventures after *Adventure*, was designed to provide not only adventure but a more literary narrative as well. It was collaboratively written by David Lebling, Marc Blank, Timothy Anderson, and Bruce Daniels while they were at MIT. Tim Anderson wrote about the beginnings of the program for The New Zork Times in 1985 (Anderson and Galley 1985).[15] Anderson's words provide insight into the tone and nature of the group's collaborative process. In creating the program they: used *Adventure* as an instigator, built preliminary prototypes, tested and reiterated, drew maps and designed problems; argued; and finally laid in a good substratum for a game to which it was easy to add new elements.

> Marc, Bruce and I sat down to write a real game. We began by drawing some maps, inventing some problems, and arguing a lot about how to make things work. Bruce still had some thoughts of graduating, thus preferring design to implementation, so Marc and I spent the rest of Dave's vacation in the terminal room implementing the first version of ZORK. ZORK, by the way, was never really named. "Zork" was a nonsense word floating around; it was usually a verb, as in "zork the fweep," and may have been derived from "zorch." ("Zorch" is another nonsense word implying total destruction.) We tended to name our programs with the word "zork" until they were ready to be installed on the system.

---

[15] A html version of The New Zork Times (Winter 1985) is at http://www.vaxdungeon.com/Infocom/Articles/NZT/Nztwin85.asp. The article is available in plain text at http://www.ifarchive.org/indexes/if-archiveXinfocomXarticles.html.

> By the time Dave got back, there was a more-or-less working game. It proba-
> bly wasn't as big as ADVENTURE, and was certainly less than half the size of
> the final version, but it had the thief, the cyclops, the troll, the reservoir and
> dam, the house, part of the forest, the glacier, the maze, and a bunch of other
> stuff. The problems were not as interesting as those that came later: it took
> time for people to learn how to write good problems, and the early parsers
> wouldn't support complicated solutions anyway. What we had done right was
> lay in the "substratum." There was a well defined (and easily changed theory
> governing interactions among objects, verbs, and rooms.
>
> It was easy to drop in new parsers, which happened frequently, since every-
> one and his uncle tried his hand at writing a parser (Marc finally became
> obsessed with it, and wrote the last 40 or 50 of them himself). And it was very
> easy to add new rooms, objects, and creatures. (I won't discuss the difficulty
> of adding new concepts yet).

In the article Anderson goes on to say that the program was improved by the
people who found and played it: "net randoms" who infiltrated the MIT systems and
created a user community. The team responded to problems that were pointed out to
them by users of the program such as "a bottomless pit in an attic should be notice-
able from the ground floor of the house" (Anderson and Galley 1985) with changes
that added to the story. Because the technology was untested, the authors were
sometimes surprised by what players were able to do with the objects they had created. Input from players was an ongoing process from the start of the project and
was welcome. User groups were part of the computer culture not only at universities
but also throughout the research community. It is a particularly charming trait of
user groups that they believed it their responsibility to improve programs, an atti-
tude that manifest itself in the open source community which became an ongoing
collaborative effort to improve online technology.

The intent of *Zork* was to simulate the real world. For the player this implied,
among other things, being able to have conversations that consisted of more than
one or two word directives like in *Adventure*. To provide for realistic conversations
the team created an advanced language parser that could analyze the text to understand the player's input. The parser examined a sentence and looked for three basic
items: verb, direct object, and indirect object, as well as other parts of speech such
as prepositions and adjectives that would help it to interpret the player intent. The
player could input a relatively complex text such as "Tie the hideous troll up with
that slimy rope." The program would break this down into verb—"tie", direct
object—"troll" and indirect object—"rope" (Briceno et al. 2000).

Because of this parser players were able to dialogue with the game in a conver-
sational tone and use contextual and personal language to engage with the narrative.
The realistic dialogue increased immersion in the story and brought with it a greater
sense of personal involvement in the collaborative creation of the narrative. Still
restricted to manipulating actions within a set network of paths, the player could,
nevertheless, be tangibly expressive through the text input while negotiating these
narrative paths. This, along with an increase in the complexity of scenarios available
to the player, again created an illusion of freedom. A level of collaboration in

authoring specific to computer programs which became manifest with *Zork*[16] was the input of the user communities who acted as "adjunct" authors and instigators to improve the program.

The creators of *Zork* went on to start the company Infocom[17] to produce text adventures commercially, the first of which was a commercial version of *Zork: Zork I*. Infocom's developers were interested in the literary quality of the games and wanted to create satisfying narratives in which players could participate (Anderson and Galley 1985). Among other genres, the company produced mystery, romance, fantasy, and science fiction stories, including an interactive version of Douglas Adam's *Hitchhikers Guide to the Galaxy*. Game writers were called Imps, short for implementors, and wrote as part of a team consisting of author, interpreter, QA (quality assurance) who worked collaboratively to create the game. Writing in 1985 about the challenge of creating well-crafted stories, Stu Galley wrote in the "Implementor's Creed":

> I create fictional worlds. I create experiences.
>
> I am exploring a new medium for telling stories.
>
> My readers should become immersed in the story and forget where they are. They should forget about the keyboard and the screen, forget everything but the experience. My goal is to make the computer invisible.
>
> I want as many people as possible to share these experiences. I want a broad range of fictional worlds, and a broad range of "reading levels". I can categorize our past works and discover where the range needs filling in. I should also seek to expand the categories to reach every popular taste.
>
> In each of my works, I share a vision with the reader. Only I know exactly what the vision is, so only I can make the final decisions about content and style. But I must seriously consider comments and suggestions from any source, in the hope that they will make the sharing better.[18]

Galley linked "creating experiences," "telling stories," and "sharing." As an author Galley took the stance that it was *his* vision he shared. As part of the team he, nevertheless, must have collaborated (considered comments and suggestions) to bring this vision (his story) to the player (to share).

Crowther had instilled *Adventure* with a sense of humor and *Zork* continued the tradition of humor. Designed on a DEC PDP-10 computer the original *Zork* could only be played by students who could access a mainframe on which it was running. The dialogue the Imps created used humor that reflected the language and culture of technology; computer engineering students attracted to playing the game were

---

[16] Earlier games probably shared a similar process. Anderson's article in which he writes about *Zork's* user groups is a convenient reference point.

[17] Infocom was founded by Tim Anderson, Joel Berez, Marc Blank, Mike Broos, Scott Cutler, Stu Galley, Dave Lebling, J. C. R. Licklider, Chris Reeve and Al Vezza.

[18] The entire *Implementor's Creed* can be found at http://web.mit.edu/6.933/www/Fall2000/infocom/creed.html.

ensured a sense of inclusion in the game narrative as they encountered inside jokes they "got." Such cultural context was a reflection of the inherent heterglossia of texts as they are adapted by authors and readers/players in collaboratively configured narratives.

Infocom's marketing packages for their games included "feelies." These were small real-world items such as the Peril Sensitive Sunglasses that were included with the manuals and disks for *The Hitchhiker's Guide to the Galaxy* and were intended to enrich the gaming experience (Barton 2007). Tangible artifacts, feelies increased the performance aspects of engagement with the game and brought the narrative out of the virtual space of the computer and into the physical space of the player. As with the manipulable paper figures in *The History and Adventures of Little Henry* book in the 1800s, feelies let players take on a persona they could enact outside the digital environment—players became performers in real space.

Infocom was responsible for popularizing the term "interactive fiction" and played a major role in bringing text adventures to the public until the market cooled at the end of the 1980s because of the emergence of graphic computer games (Montfort 2008). The evolution of the text adventure had taken a number of paths. First the genre continued as interactive fiction (IF); second it evolved into multi-user adventures (MUDs) and role playing games (RPGs). Combined with graphics these new game genres supplanted text adventures in the commercial market.

Text adventures continued to be developed by the Interactive Fiction (IF) community. Enthusiasts developed authoring systems that gave writers who were not necessarily tech savvy the tools to create their own text adventures. Technical simplicity and support from an enthusiastic group of interested players who were prepared to help with problems and then be a receptive audience for the work provided for a collaborative environment for both creating and sharing IF stories and helped grow a successful author/player community.[19] Two of these systems, *TADS*, released by Michael Roberts 1987, and *Inform*, launched by Graham Nelson in 1993, offer contemporary versions with enhanced features that make IFs even easier and faster to create today.

The other path text adventures followed was into the world of multi-users and role-playing. The first multi-user adventure in which a number of people could interact with each other in the game by typing commands was developed in 1978. Roy Trubshaw began work on the game while he was a student at Essex University. Titled *MUD* for *Multi-User Dungeon*, its development was subsequently taken over by fellow student Richard Bartle. When the university's internal network was connected to ARPANET in 1980, *MUD* became the first online multi-user adventure and the first game adventure that created a social environment in which players could interact with each other through natural language. Graphics were first added to MUDs (which became a generic name for multi-user games) in the 1988 Lucasfilm game *Habitat*. Initially called Graphical MUDs they eventually came to

---

[19] Examples of interactive fiction are available on Andrew Plotkin's *Zarf* site: http://www.eblong.com/zarf/if.html. Guides are available for writing interactive fiction at http://www.brasslantern.org/writers/howto/i7tutorial.html and http://introsteps.com/interactive-fiction/.

be known as Massive Multiplayer Online Role Playing Games or MMORPGs and offered large virtual worlds in which players could collaborate with others to strategize their way through a complex narrative.

Community of Users [Equals] Social Networks

These early forays into interactivity in storytelling in online digital environments provided for collaboration on different levels: creating the technology, writing the story, and engaging with the story. Early mediated communications such as the discussion forums that arose around interactive fiction helped establish a paradigm for dialogue as a function of narrative discourse among special interest groups. As a generation of users became comfortable with a digital environment the internet was introduced and offered a new space for expression and dialogue. The repertoire of online communication vehicles increased from email to include blogs and other social networking applications that provided an impetus for collaborative storytelling to evolve in social media—the focus of the next chapter.

Chapter 4
Storytelling on the Web: Collaborative Authoring and Social Media

Since writing was invented people have pushed new technologies to be a dialogue, both interactive and collaborative, one that not only presents but also creates knowledge.

Walter Benjamin in *The Age of Mechanical Reproduction* suggested that changes in technology offered new opportunities for cultural expression by detaching culture from traditional domains (Benjamin 1969). In the evolution of narrative in digital environments the technology permitted both traditional and a non-traditional avenues of expression. Authors could go the route of porting text and image in likeness of print;[1] they could also use digital tools to create distinct new genres. Within social media, however, the digital space did not allow easy porting of the familiar print story. Even the serial novel had to, in a blog space, accept comments. The environment itself forced alternative ways to present stories and opened avenues for exploring and redefining ideas of authoring and readership.

This chapter briefly introduces the evolution of social media sites as they have increasingly connected people, provided for sharing both personal and fictional narratives, and inspired novel narrative forms. It begins with a response to current common definitions of Web 2.0 as collaborative[2] versus Web 1.0 as static and shows that connecting people has been central to both the offline and online computer environment since its inception. The chapter then flashes through social media's growth, highlighting some key events. It shows that while the media has potential for collaboration, many of the new story genres that have emerged are turn-based, and while participatory, meet the requirements of being collaborative only modestly.

---

[1] In his article *Porting to the Web,* Richard Brandt explains "straight port" as using new technology to do things the same way as was done with the old technology during the liminal stages of development (Brandt 1999).

[2] What is Web 2.0? www.webopedia.com/TERM/W/Web_2_point_0.html.

K. Madej, *Interactivity, Collaboration, and Authoring in Social Media,*
International Series on Computer Entertainment and Media Technology,
DOI 10.1007/978-3-319-25952-9_4

An Interactive, Collaborative Environment

Today's Web is described as a virtual environment in which even a non-technical user can actively contribute content as well as interact and collaborate with others. It has been given the soubriquet Web 2.0 and is seen as the successor of Web 1.0 and computer use before WWW. The implication is that the digital environment before 2.0 consisted of static pages and users were passive viewers of these static pages. This label does not reflect the vision of connection and collaboration that inspired the direction of computer evolution or the social nature of computer environments since the 1960s. Over 70 years ago, in his 1944 article *As We May Think* Vannevar Bush described wireless data connections, voice interaction, and a memory retrieval system that necessitated *active* input and exchange of ideas. In the 1960s Doug Engelbart read this visionary statement and was inspired to innovate ways for engaging with technology at his Augmentation Research Center so that users *connected* and *collaborated* both with and through the digital environment.[3] Carrying on this spirit, Berner Lees designed the WWW in the late 1980s "to be a *collaborative* space where people can interact" and "was all about connecting people" (Laningham 2006). The introduction of user-friendly web interfaces in the mid-1990s increased the potential for the general public to use media as a collaborative space as had researchers, academics, and special interest groups such as gamers, before it.

Chapter One notes "Early communications avenues such as email and user forums, the precursors of social media, had already set a paradigm of dialogue and sharing for computer users by the 1990s." These communications systems evolved as an essential part of digital media infrastructure over the 25 years before Mosaic, launched in 1993, made browsers popular.[4] Email had been available for sending messages on a computer system's network since MIT's MAILBOX system was implemented in 1965 (Peter 2004).[5] Concepts for communications *between* computers were made reality by ARPANET[6] through a network of Interface Message Processors (IMPs); the first generation of IMPs connected four local hosts with six remote IMPs. The first message was sent from UCLA to Stanford Research Institute in October 1969 and by December four institutions were connected (Abbate 2000). The first online chat system *Talkomatic* was created in 1973 at the University of Illinois. It facilitated simultaneous messaging on six channels with up to five participants in each chat room. In 1980 the

---

[3] See www.dougengelbart.org/library/engelbart-archives.html.

[4] Mosaic was only one of a number of browsers launched around the same time. *Erwise*, a browser developed at the Helsinki University of Technology, was released earlier in April 1992, while *ViolaWWW* was released in May 1992.

[5] Email evolved from users sending messages within the same computer to users interested in communicating between computer networks. In 1972 Ray Tomlinson chose the @ symbol to denote sending messages from one computer to another: name-of-the-user@name-of-the-computer. This "nice hack" has lasted as an innovation to this day (Peter 2004).

[6] The Advanced Research Project Agency (ARPA) funded a project to create a network that allowed computer users to communicate among each other outside their own computer systems. It became known as ARPANET.

subscriber online service Compuserve released *CB Simulator* which made chat services widely available to the public. Compuserve was later joined by Prodigy and AOL, all of which still operate today. Such providers offered services that were precursors of the social networking sites that exist today on the WWW. Members created communities and joined discussions to chat with each other on topics of the day. On AOL, members could create profiles that were searchable (DigitalTrends 2014) and by 1995 CB Simulator offered channels that "enabled multiplayer games, digital pictures, multimedia, and large conferences."[7] With the likes of Mick Jagger and the Rolling Stones working with CompuServe to produce the first ever online live conference held December 1995 (PRNewswire 1995), digital media was well on its way to becoming the pervasive social phenomenon connecting people across cultures that it is today.

The mise en scène for today's use of social media's engagement with narrative was set in the early 1970s. Examples in Chapter Three identify user groups as important active participants in the development of early text adventures. Players both engaged with the adventure and also sought out other participants to discuss mutual interests. While prior to the mid-1990s hypertexts and hypermedia narratives were distributed to the public as diskettes and (then) as CD-ROMs intended for personal, individual (and unconnected) use, electronic bulletin boards facilitated discussion and collaboration within a larger community since the early 1980s. In the late 1980s HyperCard, offered free on Mac computers, gave your average, not very tech savvy author, simple tools for creating dynamic, interactive narratives that included graphics, image, and sound.

The introduction of Mosaic (1992) and Netscape Navigator (1993–1994) simplified technology for manipulating text and image in online environments. Very quickly the new *participatory* and *collaborative* digital experience moved beyond the sphere of university and corporate research into the general community and set a direction embraced by what we can now see was a public already wired and ripe for it. The use of computers was never a one-way system, before or after WWW. The purpose was always to connect people so they could access information and create knowledge through a *dialogue* with others in their interest area. The interest had at first been satisfied by local networks in research groups, then, through online networks for research and special interest groups, and finally, via free online networks for the general public. The transformation that is called Web 2.0 is not *what*, i.e. sharing and collaborating on creating knowledge, but *who*, *how*, and *how much*.

Early Online Authoring

Bulletin boards, forums, message boards, and chat services were important early forms of social media in which special interest groups shared information and participated in discussion on the internet before the WWW. Made commercially available in the late 1970s, bulletin boards had their origin in systems such as *Community Memory* which operated in several communities in Berkley, California beginning

---

[7] http://en.wikipedia.org/wiki/CB_Simulator.

August 1973, Talkomatic, which was created at the University of Illinois in 1973, and *Usenet*, which was established at the University of North Carolina and Duke University in 1980.[8] Categories (called hierarchies) and subcategories of discussion extended to millions of topics (Arendholz 2010).

In September 1983, after the collective *Invisible Seattle* completed the *Literary Computer Project*, Clair Colquitt started up the group's electronic bulletin board IN.S.OMNIA. The site became a vehicle for investigating electronic writing and hypertext throughout the 1980s and early 1990s:

> IN.S.OMNIA is a forum for interactive literature, a mode of self-publishing
> that eliminates printing presses, paper, and publishers. Call, read, write ...
> every reader is a writer, and new forms appear, a new writing that is at
> once literature, graffiti, conversation, and word games. (Wittig 1994, p. 6)

Organized around rooms in which participant members could engage in conversation with other members, the site included discussion spaces for literary themes contemporary at the time, such as Jacques Derrida and CI-NE-MA. Like the *Computer Literary Project*, the Invisibles bulletin board IN.S.OMNIA elicited both collective and collaborative writing. It included opportunities for writing individually or in a dialogue with others in "'Travesty-of-Print rooms' where writers mimic text forms such as 'Dear Abbey' or 'Reporters at Large'; 'Investigation rooms,' where the nature of data and information and text are examined; 'Workshop rooms,' where formal procedures guided by constraints are tried out" (Harris 1995). In *Invisible Rendezvous*, Wittig describes the bulletin board as a digital coffee house where members could engage in debate, collaborate on writing, and explore genres that question linearity, completion, and the single voice. He says "By its structure IN.S.OMNIA calls into question fundamental constructs of late romantic literature: the Author, the Work, the Reader" (Wittig 1994, cover flap). The bulletin board was viewed by some at the time as "a free zone for ambitious literary shenanigans" (1994).[9]

By 1995 the internet included many literary resources for authors, from bulletin boards to websites, most of which offered information and some of which offered authors ways to participate. That year, Sue Thomas of Nottingham Trent University began the Cyber-Writing Research Project to explore writing on the internet. Simon Mills, the student who searched the internet for sites, sorted what he saw as the best sites into categories and provided a review of each. The resulting publication, *Selected Internet Resource for Writers*,[10] was first produced in print. Then Mills taught himself html and created an online version that was the first entry of the trAce Writing Community website, a site that became an exploratory space for writers for the next 10 years.[11] Both the list and many of the sites it reviewed reflected Brandt's "straight port" from print and consisted of static authored works,

---

[8] Usenet was developed in 1979 and first broadcast in 1980.

[9] https://books.google.ca/books?id=l9I3AQAAIAAJ.

[10] http://tracearchive.ntu.ac.uk/writersforthefuture/1995/.

[11] http://tracearchive.ntu.ac.uk/.

or collections of authored works. However, some of the sites were more experimental and offered either collective or collaborative opportunities for participation in story creation. Two of these were *No Dead Trees*, which (from the information provided) offered a collaborative experience, and *The Walking Man*, which offered a collective experience.

No Dead Trees

http://www.acy.digex.net/~dobenson/novel_main.html

The idea is to create an interactive novel and not one in the traditional, linear plot style (dead tree).

'For the average novelist, this is an impossible task. Novels, typically written on dead trees, move in one direction ... An interactive novel, however, must be able to move in any direction at any time. To accomplish this many writers will take part in the Cybernovel.'

And you could be one of the writers.

The Walking Man

http://crow.acns.nwu.edu:8082/poeticus/walk

A collaborative visualization, a hyperfiction dreamscape ... a guy walking"

You can write it and read it. The walking man project asks you to take *him* for a walk wherever you please.

While traces of these projects can be found on the WWW, their sites existed for only a brief period. As was, and is, the case with much online material, changing technologies and a predisposition to ephemerality contained the experience. In 1994 the WWW was small enough that the appearance of new sites was presented in regularly compiled (sometimes daily, sometimes weekly) lists. *The Walking Man* project was listed in NCSA's *What's New* site for August 1994, and University of Wisconsin's *The Internet Scout* for August 26, 1994. The following newsgroup email shows the project was still generating queries about participation when it disappeared without any reference to being complete.

Newsgroups: comp.infosystems.www.misc,misc.writing
Subject: Missing in Action: Walking Man Project

There used to be a writing project called The Writing Man, about a man [who] is walking through some places. It was a group project on the World-Wide Web that was announced here some time ago. There were about 14 short stories in the project.

Well, the Walking Man seems to have walked away. The URL that used to work:

<ahref=http://daneel.acns.nwu.edu:8082/poeticus/walk/walkhome.html>
The Walking Man Project Home Page<.a>

... no longer does. It seems that daneel is no longer accessible, although this could be a local problem.

...

Does anyone know what became of the Walking Man project?

Oh well, in case anyone does, here's the story I wrote for it.

Episode 12[12]

Both of these sites had disappeared within a few years of being opened. As authors and readers came to use the internet more, resolution or completion, a hallmark of print media, was to prove a less than necessary constituent of their authoring experience in online digital media.

One of the most visible of the trAce community projects, *Noon Quilt* showed the potential to combine text with image to create a metaphorical space that was designed to reveal a collective story. TrAce sent out a request to authors around the globe to look out their window at noon and then to submit their impressions. Over 5 months during 1998–1999 Teri Hoskin and Sue Thomas collaborated on editing these text patches as in a fabric quilt.

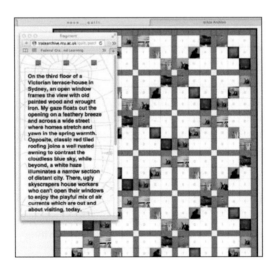

Fig. 4.1 *Noon Quilt* consisted of text impressions of locations around the world at noontime (1998–1999)

Readers could follow the growth of the quilt as each new "image" was added on the trAce website. Readers collaborated in creating new versions of the quilt each time they clicked on a patch and revealed the associated text (Fig. 4.1). The work would remain in continuous flux, never fixed, as the database of collected information could be accessed in any permutation: a peculiar attribute of collective digital narratives that *Invisible Seattle* had discovered when constructing their *Literary Computer Project* more than 15 years earlier.

---

[12] *Episode 12* can be found at http://estephenmack.com/misc/posts/oldposts/walking.txt.

Robert Coover's experimental writing project *Hypertext Hotel*, also reflected this essential permutability of the internet, a trait that forced change in the manner authors approached narrative. Coover offered his students a fictional "hotel" space in which to explore new media as a writing environment. He found his students recalcitrant, mired in writing "within the tradition of what they have read" (Coover 1992). They were forced by the multidirectional space of the internet and the accessibility to constituent parts of their story to reconsider how to approach reading and writing when provided *Hypertext Hotel* as a writing environment:

> *But confronted with hyperspace, they have no choice: all the comforting structures have been erased. It's improvise or go home. Some frantically rebuild those old structures, some just get lost and drift out of sight, most leap in fearlessly without even asking how deep it is (infinitely deep) and admit, even as they paddle for dear life, that this new arena is indeed an exciting, provocative if frequently frustrating medium for the creation of new narratives.*

In the hotel

> *writers are free to check in, to open up new rooms, new corridors, new intrigues, to unlink texts or create new links, to intrude upon or subvert the texts of others, to alter plot trajectories, manipulate time and space, to engage in dialogue through invented characters, then kill off one another's characters or even to sabotage the hotel's plumbing. (Coover 1992)*

As a collective effort, a narrative intended to have a storyline or a network of storylines could become unstable with competing intentions intruding on or undermining another author's purpose and creating chaos—"no edges … no ends or boundaries" (Coover 1992). As a collaborative effort, during which authors discussed, negotiated, and worked towards a common goal, a data mine of potential existed for the authors to create together. Coover's students "engage[d] in continuous on-line dialogue with one another, exchanging criticism, enthusiasm, doubts, speculations, theorizing, wisecracks" (Coover 1992). In addition to the collaborative nature of the students' authoring, the hypertext also offered a collaborative role to the reader. Coover quotes one of his students, Alvin Lu, "The great thing is the degree to which narrative is completely destructed into its constituent bits. Bits of information convey knowledge, but the juxtaposition of bits creates narrative. The emphasis of a hypertext should be the degree to which the reader is given power, not to read, but to organize the texts made available to her" (Coover 1992), as in drawing from and organizing a data base.

The hotel, because of changing technology at the university, became unsupportable and ended as an experiment in narrative process rather than as a completed narrative artifact.[13] Artifact remnants can still be found on the WWW for us to interpret, in the

---

[13] The Front Desk site welcomes readers to "the recently renovated Hypertext Hotel" at http://netlern.net/hyperdis/hyphotel/.

way that bits of the *Epic of Gilgamesh* (circa 2100 BCE) have been found scattered across the sands of Persia.

The internet also supported small group authoring collective/collaborations that involved only a few authors working together to create narratives, either static or interactive. The hypertext novel *The Unknown* was written and compiled between 1998 and 2002. The introductory screen, a facsimile of which follows, identifies half a dozen contributors:

THE UNKNOWN

THE ORIGINAL GREAT AMERICAN HYPERTEXT NOVEL

written by William Gillespie, Scott Rettberg, & Dirk Stratton,
with Frank Marquardt

original design by Scott Rettberg
photography and collage by Adam Richer
paintings by Katie Gilligan[14]

Scott Rettberg clarifies in his article, *All Together Now*, that Gillespie, Stratton, and he were the primary authors and "a dozen other writers and artists played some hand in its construction" (Rettberg 2005). Although rules for collection and collaboration such as *Invisible Seattle's Rules of the Game* for the *Computer Literary Project* weren't written down, the authors agreed to basic etiquette for working together: "we agreed to read the scenes that the others had written, to link to and from them when appropriate, and to allow those previously written scenes to provide a context for the scenes that we would subsequently write" (Rettberg 2005). Scenes were written both individually and composed during group sessions to which friends would occasionally be invited. The authors knew each other and were able to respond to contributions with understanding. Rettberg in particular mentions the atmosphere of play rather than "explicit agreement" or rules of engagement that guided the exploration of characters, scenes, and the spatial environment of the hypertext. As a collaboration, the project was also directed by "negotiation, confrontation, and compromise" and was as much about being able to work together as people as it was about writing (Rettberg 2005). A collaborative effort requires a goal towards which individuals work together. More than the exploration of writing which was the driving force in a project such as *Hypertext Hotel*, the group worked together to complete a hypertext novel they could present as an online narrative artifact readers would engage with and explore.

The first interactive narrative that offered an ongoing story with the intent of including readers in the evolution of the work as a learning experience as well as an authoring experience was the narrative *Inanimate Alice*.[15] Produced by Ian Harper, the narrative was created as a response to a perceived need for interactive online works for younger people, in particular those in their early teens. Young people read

---

[14] *The Unknown* can be found at http://unknownhypertext.com.

[15] http://www.inanimatealice.com.

from screens—the internet was becoming their primary narrative delivery platform. Because they played games that are narrative based, e-books, which are simply printed books ported to the web, were boring for them. They expected more dynamic content. Harper worked with writer Kate Pullinger[16] to produce an interactive narrative in which the complexity and interactivity increased progressively. The first episode of *Inanimate Alice* was released at the end of 2005. Each episode mimicked real life. As Alice, who aspired to be a game designer, grew older on the screen, her skills increased and the reader was brought along for the learning. While the series is intended for the educational market—students improve their literacy/literary/computer skills as they become a part of the collaborative effort to tell the story—the strong story inspired a fanbase of readers who followed each new episode. A screen from the educational package is shown in Fig. 4.2 (Harper 2010). *Inanimate Alice* used text, sound, music, images, videos, and games in her adventures, and introduced new technologies as the main character matured; the latest episode is being created in 3D Unity. The narrative is now in its tenth year and has started its fifth episode. The character Alice, who was initially eight, is now eighteen and has a strong Facebook presence (Fig. 4.3).[17] The young teenagers who first engaged with *Inanimate Alice* in 2005 are now young adults in their twenties whose expectations of fictional narrative are based in enjoying dynamic interaction and playing a collaborative role in creating a story.

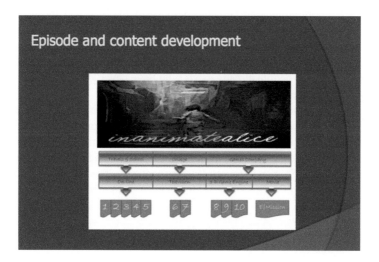

Fig. 4.2 *Inanimate Alice* Episode 1 participation tool for content development*

---

[16] Pullinger has also co-authored with Chris Joseph the collaborative online multimedia fiction *Flight Path. http://www.flightpaths.net.*

[17] https://www.facebook.com/InanimateAlice.

The BradField Company presents 'Inanimate Alice' 2010 Powerpoint presentation. Author's personal archive.

Fig. 4.3 The *Inanimate Alice* Facebook page shows it first appeared in social media in 2009

Social Media on the WWW

In the early 1990s the term "Social Media" emerged at AOL as a descriptive term used for communication products that would satisfy a need the company saw among their members: "social media, places where they can be entertained, communicate, and participate in a social environment" (Bercovici 2010).[18] The term reflected the use to which people were already putting email and discussion forums at the time but implied a broader scope. Indeed, the meaning of social media changed as the technology for communicating between individuals evolved and the numbers of people connecting through digital media exploded. In less than two decades social media has created an environment in which online dialogue through such heavily used sites as Facebook and Twitter[19] is an essential condition of our day-to-day lives. A generation of people already exists who have never known a world without the connectivity of the WWW.

The earliest social media sites migrated from online service providers as individuals and businesses found they could replace their existing commercial service provider channel with a site on the WWW at no cost. Amongst the first, if not the first, social media sites were dating sites: the domains *Kiss.com* and *Match.com* were registered in December 1994 and January 1995 respectively. The Internet already had a healthy dating culture as online subscription services promoted match sites as part of their channel line up. Soon other special interest sites such as *Classmates.com*, *CommunityConnect.com, AsianAvenue.com, BlackPlanet.com,* and *MiGente.com* where members connected, shared information, and discussed issues of interest to them were started on the WWW.

---

[18] How the term "Social Media" evolved is contested by a number of early users, including Tina Sharkey, who founded iVillage and was a business executive at AOL, and Darrell Berry who wrote a paper on "social media spaces" in May 1995.

[19] http://www.ebizmba.com/articles/social-networking-websites. eBiz lists Facebook and Twitter number 1 and 2 in the top fifteen social media sites.

One of the early social media sites that was not oriented towards a special interest group but towards social networking (like the later Facebook) was *SixDegrees*. Started in 1997, the site combined features available on other sites and became the first to use a format common in today's social networking sites: members could create personal profiles, invite friends, organize groups, message friends, and post bulletin board items to people in their friend network. The site was promoted as a way to help people connect and send messages but early users felt there was little to do once a friend request was accepted. The site lasted until 2001 (Boyd and Ellison 2008; DigitalTrends 2014).

When Jonathan Abrams created the social network *Friendster* (2002) he used features made popular by Six Degrees and also emulated those found on popular dating sites that provided the opportunity for people to look at each other's information. Abrams intent was that friends could mimic their existing real world relationships by linking their sites to the profiles of their friends. The importance of Friendster was that each time a page loaded "Friendster's servers calculated a single user's connection to other users within four degrees of separation" (Chafkin 2007). How members fit into their social network of friends, and friends of friends, was immediately visible. Initially popular, Friendster had restrictive profile regulations and alienated early users who moved on to one of the many new sites that had begun to spring up in the early 2000s, such as *MySpace*.[20]

MySpace tapped into the special interest dialogues that community-specific sites enjoyed in earlier subscriber channels by including groups excluded from Friendster, such as teens. Of particular note were the Indie Rock Bands. The fan culture and promotion around these bands quickly added a collaborative dynamic that was mutually beneficial to all factions and added to the value of connections being created online (Boyd and Ellison 2008). For many the site became a place to go daily to hang out. To many teens, who didn't know a time before the Internet, the website was as real a place as the local hangout where they could chat with their friends, check out new music, and get the latest news; in fact, it *was* the local hangout (Kornblum 2006). One feature that initially differentiated MySpace from competitors was members' ability to completely customize the look of their profiles. Members could also post music from artists and embed videos from other sites on their profiles. They were now authors of their own multimedia sites—creating a text and image persona they could add to and alter with a keystroke and then share with others.

As more social network sites based on pre-existing personal relations were adopted around the world they created a new norm of communication. Given the ease with which people could maintain their existing real life connections online, it became natural for these networks to become a part of their everyday lives and their every day conversations. Then along came Facebook with more innovative media

---

[20] Danah Boyd's essay *Friendster lost steam. Is MySpace just a fad?* provides a comparison between the two sites listing reasons for the failure of one and success of the other, i.e. Friendster's decision not to support young (teen) users because it saw itself as a dating site. See at http://www.danah.org/papers/FriendsterMySpaceEssay.html, In *How to Kill a Great Idea!* Max Chapin discusses business reasons for the failure. See at http://www.inc.com/magazine/20070601/features-how-to-kill-a-great-idea.html.

features for its members, with the now-ubiquitous "like" button, and, in 2007, with its offer of an open platform for third party developers. When Facebook entered the public domain in 2006 after 2 years as a university network (in the evolution fashion of early computer games) it had 12 million users.[21] Today it connects well over a billion members, each with their own personal narrative that is constructed of status updates, comments, photos, videos, newslinks, and conversations that are often a de facto result of the rich environment offered.

Blogs

While Facebook allowed people to write, post, and share to a network of friends and acquaintances, it was the weblog that helped spark innovations in online fiction. A weblog is a running journal, sometimes a monologue, sometimes a dialogue. It is a diary form of posting information in reverse date order that could allow for threads of discussion. While posting information and conversations were a common activity in early digital communities (Usenet, Compuserve, BBS), blogs started in 1994 when Justin Hall created his personal homepage, *Links.net*, and kept it as an online diary to share with friends, acquaintances, and followers for 11 years. An extreme form of personal blogging also initiated in 1994 was the *Lifelog* blog (http://wearcam.org/eastcampusfire), in which Steve Mann began to record his daily existence non-stop 24/7 with wearable technologies (Howard 2014; Mann 1997). The word "weblog" was introduced in 1997 by blogger Jorn Barger as a reference to his process of logging the information he browsed on the web. It was shortened to "blog" in 1999, the same year that the platform *Blogger.com* was started (Chapman 2014). Blogger was the main catalyst for inspiring the use of blogs. *Wordpress.com*, launched in 2003, is today the most used blogging network.

Growth was exponential: in 1999 there were 23 blogs on the Internet, in 2012 there were 25 billion blogging pages viewed a month.[22] Blogging became an important communication tool in connecting individuals and groups with both targeted audiences and a larger general audience, in the worlds of politics, news, and commerce. Blogs also became a favorite way to respond to mainstream and popular media sources and were used heavily to delve into topics more deeply. Within a short time they were being used to broadcast information on everything from health issues to car repairs; meta blogs, or blogs about blogs, became a ubiquitous WWW feature. Blogging wasn't just about sharing content, the comment feature made them a dialogue, a (more than) two-way communication which built community, one of the important characteristics of earlier special interest chat rooms and forums. It was the aspect of community that helped fuel blogs' incredible popularity and growth. Some bloggers received as many as 300 comments discussing an individual post.[23]

---

[21] http://www.theguardian.com/news/datablog/2014/feb/04/facebook-in-numbers-statistics.

[22] https://blogging.org/blog/blogging-stats-2012-infographic/.

[23] https://fizzle.co/sparkline/debate-should-you-allow-comments-on-your-blog-find-out-what-two-remarkably-popular-bloggers-think.

Blogs as Narrative

Blogs didn't only offer an opportunity to share personal realities, journalism, or commercial bumpf, they also offered a new platform for fiction: the framework of daily posts made them eminently suitable for serial fiction, and the inclusion of comments added opportunities for collective and collaborative works in which narratives could be co-constructed by multiple narrators.

Serial fiction is far from new. The genre was popularized by Charles Dickens in the mid-1800s with his first serial novel *Pickwick Papers*.[24] Published monthly from March 1836 until November 1837 the series proved both wildly popular and financially profitable and ensured the growth of the genre which had already been in existence for over a century.[25] Dickens continued to distribute his novels in serial form throughout his writing career, as did many other well known authors. In France Alexander Dumas's *The Count of Monte Cristo* appeared as a *feuilleton* for 139 installments and in the United States Harriet Beecher Stowe's *Uncle Tom's Cabin* was introduced to readers over a 40 week period starting on June 5, 1851. Daily and weekly strip comics and then comic books carried on the serial fiction tradition as a combination of text and image. Daily comics began to appear in newspapers in the late 1800s. The regular strip format was created in 1907 when Bud Fisher drew his *Mutt and Jeff* cartoon in a sequence across the top of one of the newspaper sections. Serial stories also translated well to early "cliffhanger" movies such as the *Perils of Pauline* (1914). Episodes in cliffhangers each told a self-contained story that ended with a precarious development or shocking revelation that only the next episode would resolve or explain. Viewers' immersion in the story secured their return for the next installment. From the 1940s on, serial fiction was adapted to television series, from short 15-minute segments primarily produced for children, to half-hour and longer episodes for adults. Serial *blog* fiction was an evolution of a story form that, in the twentieth century, had already become familiar to many people through a number of different media.

Blogs offered ways to structure information in the narrative that encouraged a collaborative approach to reading and authoring. They provided for a database architecture in which text was tagged by different categories. Authors could organize their stories in multiple ways, using both the serial capacity of the postings, as well as the link capabilities of a network of categories. While blogs were immediate and the new posts carried the narrative forward daily, links within posts gave scope to interactive niceties for readers such as access to backstories or outside links that could add to the depth or breadth of the fiction. Past posts could be archived by date, geographic place, character, or themes, and could even be grouped as chapters if the

---

[24] In 2012 Amazon announced it would offer free downloads of the serial-novel experience with Charles Dickens's *Oliver Twist* and *The Pickwick Papers*.

[25] One of the first serial narratives was the novel *Artamène* or *le Grand Cyrus* by Madeleine de Scudéry which appeared in ten volumes between 1649–1653. The number of literate people had increased steadily throughout the 1700s and 1800s and, whereas books were still expensive, publishers were able to satisfy growing demand with stories serialized in magazines and newspapers.

author wanted to provide a print paradigm for the reader. Blogs were visited daily by some readers and capriciously by other readers; because of the potential for being read by someone unfamiliar with the story, or someone who had missed a few posts, blogs best served the reader when each post was self-contained. That each post was able to function individually did not, however, preclude readers commenting on the circumstances in the post, being invited to add information in a collective fashion, or being included as collaborating authors (for the next installment for instance). Blogs were first used as personal diaries—externalized personal dialogues—and the tone of personal dialogue lingered; it shaped authors' approach to writing fiction in the blog format and readers' reactions to reading blog fiction. Blogs that were not authentic were considered to be "betraying your trust."[26]

For writers who chose to work in new digital formats blogging provided a structure that encouraged experimentation. Some authors, like Diego Doval, who was "still feeling himself around weblogs" when he began to write *Plan B* (2002),[27] created a blog fiction with the sense of a traditional serial novel. Situated in an office, the *Plan B* blog episodes took readers into the story's events through first person accounts and dialogue that created believable characters as the story was revealed. In his non-fiction personal blog[28] Doval posted about the story he was writing: his entries revealed the complexity of delivering a fiction in an environment that allowed for instant participation through comments. While comments and suggestions for story continuation or character development could be attended to in an editorial fashion within the blog fiction, comments that, for instance, questioned the pertinence of using the blog format to deliver *Plan B*, required a different approach. Doval created a FAQ that answered these types of questions for readers, and also answered questions he regularly asked himself while writing the blog. In the FAQ he notes that he addressed comments by readers about the novel content only if there were significant complaints about a specific event. Doval saw the work as a personal experiment with how the framework of a blog would affect both writing a work of fiction and the resulting narrative artifact rather than an invitation for collaborative authoring. Comments were not part of the story.

Other authors, such as Rob Wittig, who had been instrumental in sustaining the IN.S.OMNIA bulletin board as a literary space (from 1983 on), explored the blog as a new writing schema, one that in its very nature required the use of the practices of a blog. Wittig had experimented with each new literary space in this way, subverting the format and making it intrinsic to the narrative, and then taking advantage of people's expectations of the form. In 1999 Wittig had written *Friday's Big Meeting: a chatroom comedy* using a chatroom schema. The fiction was set in an office chatroom and featured a sequence of posts that were each accompanied by an image of the person posting (Fig. 4.4).

---

[26] http://www.web-strategist.com/blog/2007/10/11/list-of-flogs-astroturfing-and-fake-blogs/.

[27] http://www.dynamicobjects.com/d2r/planb/archives/2004_03_20.html.

[28] http://blog.diegodoval.com.

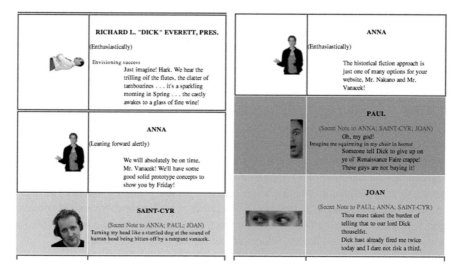

Fig. 4.4 Richard, Anna, Saint-Cyr and other employees discuss office issues in Wittig's Chatroom Comedy *Friday's Big Meeting*

This work was followed by the email narrative, *Blue Company 2002*,[29] a series of daily e-mails that Wittig sent individually and as small-group e-mails "from Berto, a marketing guy who has gotten a really bad job transfer. He's been transferred to Italy—which is great—but he's been transferred to the fourteenth century, which is uncomfortable and sometimes downright dangerous."[30] Wittig says of the process

> *The moment each day where I pressed the SEND button felt very much like a performance. Every 24-hour cycle I was imagining what was happening to the protagonist in real time so that I could write it convincingly. In my mind my narrator was a living presence in my body (like actors feel) and his words were fresh, living words, going straight to peoples' in-boxes. It was fiction sneaking into a place usually reserved for non-fiction. I hoped people were reading it at work, sneaking it into their work days.*[31]

---

[29] *Blue Company 2002* was one part of a two-part fiction. The second part, *Kind of Blue*, was written by Scott Rettberg.

[30] http://robwit.net/?page_id=141.

[31] Rob Wittig, e-mail message to author, June 30, 2015.

BlueCompany 2002 was performed twice, first in 2001, and then again in 2002 on a subscription basis.[32] In 2002 Wittig started the fictional blog *robwit.net*.[33] The blog featured entries made by Wittig and two fictional friends. The posts delineate the friendship within a real world context that was established through outside links. Reader comments were enabled; as Wittig responded to these, the blog fiction, rather than being scripted, emerged.

While such blog fictions are considered akin to epistolary novels such as *Dracula* (1897), in which Bram Stoker made use of journal entries, letters, telegrams, and memos—the personal communication technologies of the day—to provide verisimilitude to his story, given Wittig's blog is fiction adopted-to-reality, a more apt analogy would have the Dracula story featured in *The Times of London* in a series of "real" articles to which readers could respond by sending letters to the editor to comment on events. In the days of early Victorian newspapers, that participation would have been a collaboration between the journalist and the reader, true in particular if the reader's letters influenced the direction of future articles.

Blogs successfully bridged into popular print literature. Brook Magnanti, who had started the blog *Diary of a London Call Girl* under the nom de plume Belle de Jour in 2003, was offered "six-figure advances" from publishers who wanted to sign her on because of the runaway success of the blog (McClellan 2004). Magnanti, a graduate student, began her blog in October 2003 and continued writing under that pseudonym until November 2009 when her real identity was revealed. When the blog won the Guardian newspaper's Best British Weblog for 2003, Belle de Jour was viewed as manipulating the blog genre to her advantage as vanity publishing: "Archly transgressive, anonymous hooker is definitely manipulating the blog medium, word by word, sentence by sentence far more effectively than any of her competitors … . She is in a league by herself as a blogger" (Waldman 2003).

The publishing success of a narrative both as an online blog and as a print book effectively demonstrates the transmedia nature of narrative: the same stories adapt to different communications technologies readily. Lulu, the self-publishing company started in 2002, has, since 2006, bestowed the Lulu Blooker Prize for the best "blook" of the year, the narrative which began as a blog fiction and was then successfully adapted to print. As a blog, the fiction was open to comments, serialization, and change. As a book, the fiction became a "reified" text, one that could no longer undergo change (remember Socrates comments on dialogue being critical to us as thinking human beings?). The book was, in effect, a slice of the ongoing world of the blog.

---

[32] *Blue Company 2002* was "arguably the first epistolary email narrative to be written and published for paying e-mail subscribers in real time." http://www.nytimes.com/2004/04/15/technology/call-me-e-mail.html.

[33] robwit.net is no longer fictional, but a space which hosts Wittig's personal blog and where he maintains all of his digital works.

Such fiction is sometimes given short shrift by the academic community as a "popular" literary genre, not worthy of serious study. Notwithstanding such opinions, Blog Fiction gained so much traction with the general public that today Goodreads, the world's largest book review site,[34] includes a page for authors and readers of online serial fiction that encourages participation in both submitting works and discussing them.

> Do you blog a story? Read web comics or online serial fiction? Let's explore the serial medium and discuss what makes serial fiction so much fun. Authors, how can we keep em reading? Fans, what do you want from your favorite serial stories?

Hundreds of sites now offer formulaic serial fiction methods for writing a blog-fiction. Many promote the "collaborative" nature of the serial fiction for which they provide writing advice. Fortunately experimentation with the form also continues.

Twitter

However popular blogs were at the time, it was the microblog Twitter that sparked a major wave of interest in authoring fiction—individual, collective, and collaborative—in social media. A microblog is a short form blog with a restriction on the number of words/characters that can be posted. In the case of Twitter, users posted 140 characters at a time. Initially only text could be posted. Twitter was used as a newsfeed for following those who are well-known, as a pseudo-chatroom (by limiting followers and who was followed), and as a microblog for updating others on life/work events. Almost from its start in 2006, Twitter was also used as a new form for telling stories, both personal and fictional.

Larry Smith and Rachel Fershleiser launched the online magazine *SMITH* in January 2006 with the belief that everyone has a story they want to tell. They planned for the magazine to be populist and participatory: users (not necessarily professional writers) would generate the content and editors would curate it. Early in the career of the magazine, a lead story fell through and they replaced it with an idea for a new type of story.

> *We quickly popped in a new idea we had been kicking around: giving Hemingway's legendary six-word novel ("For sale: baby shoes, never worn") a personal twist. We combined the classic storytelling challenge with our passion for nonfiction confessionals and dubbed it "Six-Word*

---

[34] "Goodreads is the world's largest site for readers and book recommendations. We have more than 40 million members who have added more than 1.1 billion books … ." http://www.goodreads.com/about/us.

*Memoirs." Then we called up some guys we met at a tech conference about
this new thing called Twitter and asked if they wanted to partner up to send
one daily short life story to anyone who followed our @smithmag feed.
(Smith 2010)*

Twitter's 140 character limit suited the new project and *Six Word Memoirs* was
launched.[35] Setting the boundary of six words created the challenge for writers to
get to the essence of their ideas. The topic "memoir" provided a framework for writers, but it was sufficiently encompassing that writers could consider anything from
daily news reports to taking vacations as long as it was associated with a past aspect
of their lives. Within 4 years, over 200,000 *Six-Word Memoirs* had been submitted.
The audience was so diverse that a site just for teens as well as one for teachers were
also launched. Smith and Fershleiser found a major benefit of the online magazine
was the community that evolved around it: diverse, passionate, and interested in
participating in the form and in a dialogue about the form (Smith 2010).

Twitter had increasingly come to the attention of authors as an opportunity for
exploring writing, and as a way to connect, both amongst themselves and with readers. In 2008 a group of published authors started the online *Book View Café* as a
cooperative for the specific purpose of connecting directly with their readers via the
internet. The *Café* opened its Twitter account in June[36] and launched its website site
in November that year. The website collected and featured "stories, poetry, a
screenplay and episodes from serialized novels for free," [37] a blog on which authors
talked about writing fiction, and, for the first couple of years, regularly scheduled
Twitter Fiction contests. The *Café* launched its first contest 5 months after the site
opened, April 10th 2009. "The task: to write a complete story incorporating the
contest theme in one tweet (126 characters or fewer). The Theme: Elf meets
vampire."[38] The extra characters (i.e. to make up 140), were intended for the hashtag.
The contests continued with different themes throughout 2009–2010. The theme of
the 6th Twitter fiction contest (September 2009) was *Fairy Tale Noir.* The judges,
Seanan McGuire, Pati Nagle, and Phyllis Irene Radford chose the following two
winning entries:

> talkstowolves @ bookviewcafe
> "You got in the way of a good thing grandma," she said, as her lover's canines
> snapped tight on old flesh and housecoat all.

> SaladOfDoom @ bookviewcafe
> I had her proof, but she wasn't going to like my report. The prince really did
> have a mistress … And tadpoles.

---

[35] https://twitter.com/sixwords?lang=en.

[36] https://twitter.com/bookviewcafe.

[37] http://www.theguardian.com/books/booksblog/2008/nov/19/fiction-sciencefictionfantasy
andhorror.

[38] http://www.bookviewcafe.com/index.php/BVC-First-Ever-Twitter-Fic-Contest.

As with the magazine *SMITH*, *Café's* appeal was both as a place to feature fiction, as well as a discussion space where authors could discuss writing, plan project and events, or collaborate on writing. After the initial interest in Twitter, the magazine turned to publishing more traditional forms of story.

An early fiction publication site devoted totally to writing on Twitter, *Nanoism*, got its start when the author Ben White saw a New York times article on the Twitter/ Mad Men/AMC kerfuffle (see later in this section). As an author who already wrote Flash fiction[39] he was inspired to use Twitter as a platform to create one-tweet stories. He found that there were others doing the same thing and, to grow the community, started Nanoism in 2009 (McMillan 2012). The magazine continues to bring authors and readers together today. The intro reads:

> Shorter than traditional flash fiction, it's both a challenge to write and quick as a blink to read. Call it nanofiction, microfiction, twiction, twisters, or tweet-fic—it doesn't matter: It's the perfect art form for the bleeding edge of the internet revolution.[40]

Twitter supported the challenge of the six-word memoir, the single tweet story, and serial fiction, but as a microblog it had more to offer: interaction between Tweeters. Dylan Meconis, an Oregon-based cartoonist, accidently create "the first narrative to truly explore the interactive potential of Twitter as a medium." Meconis "loved text-based games" and was interested in experimenting with more spontaneity in her writing (McMillan 2012). In June 2008 Meconis opened @DameJetsam[41] and posted

> ... diary excerpts from an anonymous shipwreck victim who's just washed ashore on an abandoned island, gradually building up to [reveal] that this person was female, young, and was a prisoner being transported either to or from the Australian penal colonies in the nineteenth century. (McMillan 2012)

Meconis was surprised when other Twitter users created characters for the story and joined in to develop it further. Eventually there were three other collaborating authors, including "Sir Flotsam" and "Dr. O. Detritus, some of whom posted as multiple characters. Over several months a successful Victorian supernatural romance evolved, with Meconis not knowing who the collaborators were or being in contact with them except through the Twitter posts. The opportunity to collaborate anonymously appears to be unique to social media. *Exquisite Corpse* and other experimental collaborative constructs aside, collaboration amongst authors usually implied creating a relationship and connecting over the work, as in the construction of the hypertext *The Unknown*, in which authors negotiated, confronted, and compromised (Rettberg 2005). Collaboration for *Dame Jestsam* on the other hand, was a collaboration of authors through the text. Each author read what had been written

---

[39] Flash fiction is very short fiction. The idea has translated well to *Twitter*.

[40] http://nanoism.net.

[41] https://twitter.com/damejetsam.

by the other authors and, based on their understanding of where the story was going, contributed their text. One of the reasons for *Dame Jetsam's* success was its use of the medium as more than just a sequential story delivery engine (Rettberg 2005). Meconis used Twitter to write fiction as she would use it to communicate to her friends and readers, as a co-constructed conversation that was constantly evolving. The construction of the narrative was not in any one person's control, rather, the story unfolded as a result of the author's understanding the conventions of the medium and using them to support the narrative.

At the beginning of August 2008, fictional characters from the television hit *Mad Men*[42]—Don Draper, Peggy Olsen, Roger Sterling, and others—appeared on Twitter and began to tweet one another about events on the show, creating, in effect, a second online world for the agency.[43] Initially, AMC asked Twitter to close the accounts, but an angry response from readers quickly had the characters back, recreating their agency relationships. In his writings Bakhtin had emphasized that the way we think about and use language was shaped by centralizing official tendencies, but that at the same time there existed a "dialogized heteroglossia" in the folk events of the general public that unsettled it. He said "Language lives only in the dialogic interaction of those who make use of it" (Morson and Emerson 1990, p. 130). This brief but revealing series of events showed the heterglossic nature of a new media such as Twitter in which official forces wanted to impose order on what was essentially a messy world, while unofficial forces continually disrupted that order—and continued to change and shape our language.

During the summer of 2009, the Royal Opera House, as part of ROH2 the contemporary programming arm, experimented with using Twitter as a large-scale collaborative venture to explore opera as a living art form and make it accessible to everyone. The public was invited to participate in composing the libretto, the text or script, for *Twitterdammerung: The Twitter Opera,* which was to be written entirely of tweets.[44] The first line of the opera was posted on the @youropera Twitter page—"One morning, very early, a man and a woman were standing, arm-in-arm, in London's Covent Garden. The man turned to the woman and he sang ..." After some confusion and consultation ROH found it would be better to tweet to a hashtag and people were asked to tweet to #youropera (Fig. 4.5).[45] Participants read the most current tweets, considered the direction of the storyline, and added their suggestion/s. By the end of the month-long project more than 2000 people had tweeted additions to the plotline.[46]

---

[42] *Mad Men* first aired July 19, 2007.

[43] *http://www.businessinsider.com/2008/8/amc-to-twitterers-please-don-t-market-madmen-for-us.*

[44] The complete libretto can be accessed on the Royal Opera House website at http://www.roh.org.uk/news/twitter-opera-the-libretto-so-far-plus-who-wants-to-be-on-channel-4-news. The prologue is reproduced in Chapter 7.

[45] Hashtags, which turn the words after them into a searchable link, first appeared in 2007. By 2009 they were regularly being used to search for content. When a participant clicked #youropera they were directed to the correct twitter site to post their submissions.

[46] http://www.corpcommsmagazine.co.uk/awards/digi/winning-entries/1060-best-use-of-twitter.

Fig. 4.5 The Royal Opera House includes a hashtag for its *The Twitter Opera*

The Opera's director John Lloyd Davies, edited the tweets and together with the two composers, Helen Porter and Mark Teitler, constructed an "actually watchable, listenable and rather funny opera."[47] Much of the music was original and composed during the 3 days before the performance. Porter explains that once she realized there wasn't a traditional plot line to present, she could relax and enjoy the project for what it was, experimental and spontaneous: "It's the fastest I ever worked—it's quite liberating."[48] In response to the text, the music included many references to and parodies of existing operas. The final performance was held in an informal setting at the Royal Opera House during the Deloitte Ignite Festival. It drew over 3700 people, including children, many who had not attended an opera previously (Fig. 4.6). Twenty laptops were made available during the performance so that participants could tweet suggestions during the performance.[49] The combination of participation in the initial creation of the opera through Twitter and the subsequent attendance of the performance of that creation, brings into sharp relief the dialogic nature of the event, and makes visible Bakhtin's theories about the active and social nature of narrative (Morson and Emerson 1990). Alison Duthie, who runs the contemporary program at the ROH commented: "It's the people's opera and the perfect way for everyone to become involved with the inventiveness of opera as the ultimate form of storytelling."[50] An example of the tweeted libretto can be found in Chapter 7.

---

[47] http://www.washingtonpost.com/wp-dyn/content/article/2009/09/06/AR2009090602317.html.

[48] http://www.corpcommsmagazine.co.uk/awards/digi/winning-entries/1060-best-use-of-twitter.

[49] http://www.telegraph.co.uk/technology/twitter/6004758/The-Twitter-Opera-new-Royal-Opera-House-production-in-tweets.html.

[50] http://www.channel4.com/news/articles/arts_entertainment/performing_arts/opening+night+for+the+twitter+opera/3332657.html.

Fig. 4.6 *Twitterdammerung: The Twitter Opera* performance at Covent Garden with Hannah Pedley and Andrew Slater. Photo John Lloyd Davies

Inspired by this success, BBC Audiobooks America asked the award-winning author Neil Gaiman to experiment with a crowd-sourced audio fiction using Twitter as a platform. Gaiman tweeted the words:

> Sam was brushing her hair when the girl in the mirror put down the hairbrush, smiled, and said, 'We don't love you anymore.'[51]

10,000 lines were tweeted in response over the next 8 days: each was read and tweet-by-tweet the narrative was edited into the fairytale *Hearts, Keys, and Puppetry*. The final version included 874 tweets from 124 contributors (Ohannessian 2009) and was recorded as an audio book that can be downloaded for free.[52] Promoted as "a collaborative audiobook written by Neil Gaiman and the 'Twitterverse'" (Fig. 4.7), the novel was, rather, *collectively* authored by the crowd and *collaboratively* constructed by the editors. Participants had the opportunity to read what had already been written and to be thoughtful about what they contributed but they weren't given the agency to make decisions that created the final version of the story. Editors made those decisions as the tweets were posted. Participants whose tweets were chosen did receive acknowledgement and thanks from BBC for their contribution. In the spirit of Twitter immediacy they could tweet the audio timestamp of their "lines" to friends and followers, who could then listen for those lines (Rudin 2011).

---

[51] https://twitter.com/neilhimself/status/4837873679.

[52] Audio book available free at http://www.sffaudio.com/?p=13878.

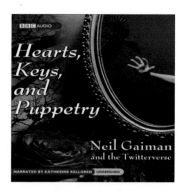

Fig. 4.7 BBC Twitter novel *Hearts, Keys, and Puppetry* composed by Neil Gaiman and the "Twitterverse"

The term "collaborative" was increasingly being used to describe participatory turn-based online story construction. In this book collaboration has been used to describe relationships between authors and text, readers and text, authors and readers, authors and authors, as well as between larger numbers of individuals in production teams. There would seem to be sufficient flexibility to include collective, aggregate efforts under the term collaborative. The difference is in the process. Collaboration requires more than the accretion of sequential posts (no matter how thoughtful these may be), it requires active negotiation to construct those posts into a final work. This is possible in turn-based environments, as Meconis's *@DameJetsam* has shown, but poses a difficult logistical challenge when there are large numbers of participants, as in crowd-sourced narratives. The company Grammarly successfully took on the challenge of a crowd-sourced novel as a collaborative authoring experience, albeit not a turn-based Twitter novel.

Grammarly crowd-sourced the novel *The Lonely Wish-Giver* during National November Writing Month in 2013. A call for participants brought forth 300 writers from 27 countries.[53] With a large collaborative project, it is important that contributors' roles and the rules or constraints of the project be clearly defined (Rettberg 2005), in the way, for instance, that *Invisible Seattle* defined the *Rules of the Game* for its 1983 *Computer Literary Project.* For *The Lonely Wish-Giver,* Grammarly assigned 25–26 writers to each of the 30 chapters planned for the book. Writers received their chapter as a Google Document and were asked to write as little as one sentence or up to 800 words, but only on the day they were assigned to do so. They could share feedback and editing comments on Facebook pages set up for each chapter. They could also post comments on Google Doc. Once the chapter was written, two authors from each chapter were asked to edit their chapter for consistency; Grammarly's team did the final edit. While not every author had a say in the final

---

[53] http://www.grammarly.com/blog/2014/grammowrimo-breaking-news/.

editing for the book, there was discussion and negotiation amongst each group of authors, and then between the two author/editors. The final novel was published as an ebook in April 2014. Grammarly successfully repeated the collaborative project the next year and in April 2015 published the crowd-sourced *Frozen by Fire*, a novel about Pompeii, that was written by 500 writers from 54 countries. Crowd sourcing has become a common call-to-action for participating in writing short stories, novels, and other forms of fiction, whether through a writing blog, Facebook, Twitter, or other social media platform.

Image-based social media sites now add to people's opportunities to engage in visual dialogue and share their stories through image on the WWW. Reflecting current ideas about image sites, a recent Huffington Post article noted that blogging is evolving "from text-based content to a visually-rich medium" and that this "marks a transformation in the thought process of society." The article notes that in 2012 there was

> *... a pronounced shift in content consumption with the rise of Tumblr, Pinterest and Instagram. In fact, a study that year found that 44 percent of users were more likely to engage with a brand that posts photos rather than purely text-based content … . And it makes sense: visual information is more quickly processed than other types of content … . in today's mobile world, people are more attracted to pictures and visual graphics than anything else.[54]*

What seems to be forgotten in this statement is that image has been a primary way to share information for millennia. Text literacy is a relatively new phenomenon: literacy rates didn't start rising until the eighteenth century when, in England as an example, they increased to about 65% of the population. By the mid-1800s, even as text became increasingly important, *illustrated* newspapers and magazines were common, photography was an up-and-coming medium of expression, and posters and billboards were used extensively to promote commercial events. By the end of the 1800s film was also well on its way to establishing itself as a ubiquitous image-based narrative medium. One notable example of image-based narrative comes from the first third of the twentieth century. Magazine publisher Henry Luce believed people had an affinity for stories told through images. He purchased *Life Magazine* in 1936 and specifically gave it a strong photojournalism emphasis. As the first all-photographic news magazine in the USA, *Life* became a staple in people's homes, selling as many as 13.5 million copies a week at one point. As of the 1950s television entered homes and continued to feed a love of image to tell stories. In print, graphic novels emerged as a significant new genre. In digital media, there isn't a website today that doesn't rely on image to tell its story. It is disingenuous to be surprised at society's continued interest in image as story and to think that image-based social media programs are changing our thought process. It is the media that has caught up to our interest rather than vice versa.

---

[54] http://www.huffingtonpost.com/andre-bourque/is-collaborative-storytel_b_5977988.html.

In addition to *Tumblr, Pinterest,* and *Instagram,* sites such as *Flickr, YouTube, SnapChat* and one of the latest iterations, *Pheed,* that describes itself as "a free social multimedia platform that enables users to create, inspire and share text, photos, videos, audio tracks, voice-notes and live broadcasts,"[55] have added to a growing panoply of ways to connect, share, dialogue, and, sometimes, collaborate. In the end, what these generate in new forms and media are the conversations and "plurality of language" that have always been a part of our culture (Calvino 1993).

Part I of this book has presented interactive narrative artifacts from the past millennium and shown the opportunities for engagement and collaboration they offered. Part II shares the dynamic process of collaboration a team of six students engaged in to create an interactive narrative work that unfolded through social media.

---

[55] https://www.pheed.com.

Part II
Interactive Narrative: Collaborative Practice

The word in living conversation is directly, blatantly, oriented toward a future answer-word: it provokes an answer, anticipates it and structures itself in the answer's direction. Forming itself in an atmosphere of the already spoken, the word is at the same time determined by that which has not yet been said but which is needed and in fact anticipated by the answering word. Such is the situation with any living dialogue. The orientation towards an answer is open, blatant and concrete.

—The Dialogic Imagination: Four Essays
Mikhail Bakhtin

Chapter 5
Romeo and Juliet on Facebook:
After Love Comes Destruction

The Future of the Book/the Book of the Future

Romeo and Juliet on Facebook had its origin in my study of Mikhail Bakhtin's *The Dialogic Imagination: Four Essays* which I first read when doing graduate research in digital narrative. The phrase, "The word in living conversation," stayed with me as a distillation of Bakhtin's ideas on dialogism and heteroglossia: ideas particularly pertinent to a study of narrative's adaptation to different media. I had an abiding interest in historical narrative artifacts, and that shaped my view of narrative. I saw it as millennia of storytelling with humans reinterpreting their stories over time, pushing the evolution of the narrative along with the evolution of technology. Dialogism, and Kristeva's take on it, intertextuality, were, today, made tangible in the mashups prevalent in the websites, blogs, and social media sites my students and I visited daily.

During one of the presentations of students' work I regularly attended at Georgia Tech[1] I was drawn to one demonstration that featured a Facebook page showing Romeo and Juliet images from familiar movies and a timeline entry that epitomized a contemporary take on the fated lovers' story (Fig. 5.1):

The page was part of a project submitted for an English Composition course during the Fall 2012 semester taught by Dr. Aaron Kashtan. Kashtan, a Britain Fellow and scholar of media, comics and materiality, assigned the project "The Future of the Book/the Book of the Future" to students so they would both theorize on the future of the book and develop a narrative artifact that reflected their ideas of what

---

[1] I teach in the School of Literature, Media, and Communication (LMC) at Georgia Tech. The Writing and Communication Program at LMC delivers Georgia Tech's Composition Courses that all students must take and that introduce them to rhetoric, process, and multimodality. The courses are taught primarily by the Brittain Postdoctoral Fellows. Students taking the courses are expected to innovate and produce projects that break new ground. At the end of each semester they put their work on display for the entire University body to engage with.

© The Author(s) 2016
K. Madej, *Interactivity, Collaboration, and Authoring in Social Media*,
International Series on Computer Entertainment and Media Technology,
DOI 10.1007/978-3-319-25952-9_5

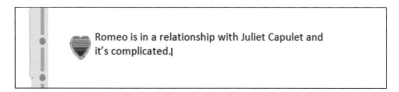

Fig. 5.1 Facebook relationship meme: contemporary commentary on *Romeo and Juliet*

a book of the future would look like. In what was to me the most intriguing of all the projects, this team of students had considered how a story could be written using the communication technologies with which they were familiar, and chose to adapt the story of *Romeo and Juliet* to the social media site Facebook. *Romeo and Juliet*, a young couple's story of love and miscommunication, seemed tailor-made for a medium that was used so ubiquitously to share personal narratives. The students accommodated the story—its plot, characters, and setting—to the medium. The Facebook format provided for photos, maps, events, and an ongoing dialogue through posts that carried the storyline. Using common mashup[2] techniques, and borrowing heavily from popular Romeo and Juliet movies, students sketched out each character to include friends, groups, books, music, sports, and other likes/interests on the pages they constructed.

Fig. 5.2 *Romeo and Juliet*: Facebook narrative as "Future of the Book"

Figure 5.2 shows the group's Facebook page of Romeo Montague with the timeline displayed. As friends, the three characters they had made pages for, Romeo, Juliet, and Rosaline, would see each other's posts and any events in which they would have participated together.

---

[2] A mashup mines existing text and imagery and combines it to create a new entity, much like a DADA collage.

The students had adapted a canonic piece of literature to a medium that reflected contemporary trends in interactive story and social media engagement. This version of *Romeo and Juliet* had a sense of the complexity of hypermedia novels that presented narrative through a network of text, image, and dialogue; it used Facebook's database structure for presenting backstory information; it took advantage of social media forms to deliver the story; and it used social media practices to engage in the collaborative authoring process. Here was dialogism reflected through a contemporary and culturally contextual narrative mashup.

Adapting Narrative Collaboratively

I'd been following the trajectory of interactive narratives and the collaborative nature of these narrative artifacts across history; the student's work before me was the manifestation of an adaptation of an old story to a contemporary medium. The nature of the project offered potential for exploring a number of my interests further: the *Romeo and Juliet on Facebook* project began to take shape.[3] In addition to exploring the process of adapting existing narrative works to a social media space, I wanted to experiment with small group collaboration in authoring in that space. The final product would be an interactive narrative based on a canonical, or at least recognized, piece of literature. The intent was to create an environment for people to experience a literary work they enjoyed not only as readers but also as collaborative authors: to let them play with the affordances of social media to bring their vision of the story into a hyper-mediated space where they could engage with it as text, image, video, and sound. The point was to author with a group of like-minded friends or colleagues in a social media setting (like a book club)—but to explore the author rather than the reader/player experience. Whether this could be a literary experience that engaged participants sufficiently to want to repeat it after more than one book was a question to be asked after the first step: try it out. As Benjamin said in "The Age of Mechanical Reproduction," changes in technology offer new opportunities for cultural expression, and social media would detach the narrative from its traditional moorings and alter the way the group would engage with its production (Benjamin 1969).

In *A Theory of Adaptation* scholar Linda Hutcheon discusses one of the purposes of adaptation as bringing a story from a previous generation into a current context so that a contemporary audience can relate to it more readily (Hutcheon 2012). Using this viewpoint, and interactive social media as a narrative environment, the group's task would be to approach the story's development as a digital media production, one that addressed all three aspects of narrative as material culture: content—plot, character, and setting within cultural context; form—structures for presenting the content; and the media—the final interaction with the audience.

---

[3] The literal title was purposeful not just happenstance; it reflected the immediate and personal nature of the story.

While the intent of the project did not include reaching a larger audience, i.e. it would be sufficient to engage with the story themselves, some thought to the story's online presence and its accessibility by an audience, given the social media context, would be useful to consider.

Facebook seemed a good choice as a starting point because using it required no new technology, because it was ubiquitous and facilitated multimedia dialogue, and because of its data base capabilities. The size of the collaborating group would be modeled on the original tabletop *Dungeon and Dragon* games—which consisted of a small number of individuals interested in carrying a particular story forward amongst themselves.[4] In this I was also inspired by book clubs. While book clubs can conjure visions of fashionable social forums at which popular fiction is discussed, they are, basically, a participatory environment for discussion, analysis, and sharing of ideas about fiction (or other narrative) in a social setting. One could conjecture that the popularity of online social environments such as chatrooms and blogs created a predisposition to a participatory approach for engaging with fiction that has, in the tangible world, manifest itself in the physical setting of the book club. But whatever the reason, book clubs have grown exponentially over the past 20 years. In her article *The Book Club Phenomenon*, Katie Wu notes that in 1990 there were 50,000 book clubs in the US; by 2000 there were at least 100,000. She goes on to say that a Google search for book clubs in 2003 resulted in 424,000 hits, while today a search of "Book Clubs in the USA" results in 29 million hits. Even if many of these are duplicates or search engine references, the result indicates an interest in a shared participation in engaging in discussion about stories.[5] But getting back to size of the group: while even locally situated book clubs can have as many as 40 people, group dynamics research shows that 6–12 people is an optimum size to offer opportunities for interaction and discussion yet retain cohesion and ability to identify with one another, important considerations for the collaboration I envisioned.[6]

I used a number of opportunities over 3 years to explore collaborative authoring affordances in social media. The first project, described in detail in this chapter, required students to collaborate on adapting Shakespeare's play *Romeo and Juliet* over 12 weeks in an Advanced Narrative course at the Center for Digital Media in Vancouver. Taking into consideration the outcomes of this first course, I restructured the project for a larger group of undergraduate students in the Narrative Across Media course at Georgia Tech in Spring 2014. In that case, four teams of students adapted four different stories, *Eighty Days Around the World, Dracula, The Great Gatsby*, and *Where'd You Go Bernadette?* I repeated the project in 2015 for an

---

[4] *D&D* groups range from 3 to 8 players with most desirable around 5. See at http://www.reddit.com/r/DnD/comments/1z42ey/whats_your_ideal_group_size/.

[5] http://www.mcsweeneys.net/articles/the-book-club-phenomena.

[6] http://www.referenceforbusiness.com/management/Gr-Int/Group-Dynamics.html.

http://www.faculty.londondeanery.ac.uk/e-learning/small-group-teaching/group-dynamics-how-group-size-affects-function.

Interactive Narrative course with a small group of students, again at CDM, and used the book *Where'd You Go Bernadette?* Each of the iterations showed that today's communication media, whether Facebook or Slack (used at CDM in 2015), are oriented towards a participatory mode of interaction and provide supportive conditions for collaboration. Once responsibilities were distributed each member of a group could work individually to create components (text, images, media) and as a team to bring the components together dynamically. Because of the academic environment, each group had had previous experience in working in teams; whether the way they shaped their collaborative experience in social media would translate into a more general environment, where such experience may not be common, is a question not yet addressed. The basic model of using readily available social media technologies and practices and applying these to the creation of literary artifacts resulted in successful collaboration and dynamic narratives in all three projects. While canonical works might not retain their importance in the form of print text, these projects show that their adaptation to contemporary social media forms is certainly realizable.

The first iteration for a 12-week project at CDM was planned with four stages:

Phase I Project preplanning and planning (Week 1–2)

> Theme and media discussion
> Narrative genre and tone
> Set up platform for collaboration
> Read the book

Phase II Storyline (Week 3–5)

> Team responsibilities and roles
> Create group Facebook page
> Plan story, plot main action
> Chose characters and determine main character traits, set up individual Facebook
>   pages
> Plan main character interactions and social media platforms
> Finalize Schedule

Phase III Background research and world building (Week 6–10)

> Research history, politics, religion, business, environment, arts
> Character development
>
>> Individually: develop database of assets revealing character's personality.
>>   Draft suggested interactions with other characters.
>> As team: Review interactions between characters for consistency and develop
>>   final artifacts.

World development

Individual: determine characters' interactions with world events, create
images/text for exploring
As team: finalize tone/graphic choices, check consistency between characters'
sites

Media: create library of assets: documents, objects, sites. Upload to repository

Phase IV Project Presentation and Review (Week 11–12)

Finalize story assets and test story delivery
Present story as a team
Discuss, critique
Debrief, comments about class

Center for Digital Media

Stage 1 Project Preplanning

The Center for Digital Media in Vancouver is a digital media school that offers an
18-month professional degree Masters program based on the Carnegie Mellon ETC
Master of Entertainment Technology. At CDM graduate students are offered a core
curriculum that includes Foundations of Digital Media, Interdisciplinary
Improvisation, The Visual Story, Building Virtual Worlds, and Foundations of
Game Design. After this they undertake real world projects and advanced courses in
subjects such as game design and narrative. By their third term students have already
been involved in a number of team projects, at least one of them client based, and
have experienced the dynamic of working collaboratively to utilize their specific
skill sets as part of a directed whole.

George Johnson, a film producer with extensive credentials in documentary
films, was the main instructor for narrative courses at CDM and welcomed new
ideas for the course we would be teaching together. I suggested that for one of the
class projects students could enact a classic story using social media affordances to
explore storytelling possibilities—this would offer them an opportunity to explore
interactive narrative in culturally contextual ways. At the time my take was that
students could create a story together that included a story site and individual character sites with information streams nuanced to character's different intentions.
There could be maps showing locations of interactions, photos and videos as background or revelation, friends, groups, likes, comments, links and rss feeds to reflect
the ongoing action. The timeline could present key juncture points in the narrative.
The project could also entail looking at how the story had been treated in other
media as a comparison. This could be done as a small or large group project.
Possible narratives were Shakespeare's play *Romeo and Juliet* or Carroll's fantasy

Alice in Wonderland, which has comedic and ironic overtones and potential for exaggeration in the Facebook environment.

Johnson was very receptive to the idea. He suggested that a story such as *Romeo and Juliet* would be easier for the students to work with as the "constraints and restrictions" of a defined plot would prompt creative experimentation. *Alice* would be too open-ended and would offer too many options from which to choose for the short period of time the students had for the project. After some discussion the final project was defined further. Rather than adapting Shakespeare's *Romeo and Juliet* extant to an interactive environment, the assignment would require students to extend the original story from 6 months after the deaths of the lovers.

Introducing the Concept

The intent of the CDM Advanced Narrative summer course is to provide graduate students with opportunity to experience aspects of digital narrative not addressed in the Visual Story course. The class meets 3 hours a week for 13 weeks with final presentations the second to last week and a debriefing the last week. In 2013 the course started on May 9 and concluded on August 8. Six students officially registered for the class and four students audited for a total of ten. Only the six registered students participated fully in the projects and received grades; everyone participated in discussions and was asked to provide comments.[7]

The focus of the course was to look at and gain an appreciation of story structures of different narrative genres and how these might be useful in creating interactive narratives. In addition to lectures by George on narrative structure in film and my lectures on narrative structure across media throughout history, there were two major assignments: a presentation and a group project. The presentation was a structural analysis of a plot from a work of the student's choice. For the group project students were offered three alternatives, one of which was the social media option:

(a) Research project: to research and analyze the major changes made in the adaptation of the print novel *Lord of the Rings* into first a film and then a game.
(b) Research/pre-production project: to analyze the novel *Cloud Atlas*, design an interactive narrative, and create a prototype.
(c) Production project: to create an interactive novel in a social media environment based on Shakespeare's *Romeo and Juliet*. The project description read in part:

> It is the 6-month anniversary of the death of Romeo and Juliet. Call them what you will, situate them in time and space as you like, but it is their story, as defined by Shakespeare, that drives this project.
>
> A series of websites, blogs, FaceBook pages, Flickr, Tumblr, Twitter feeds, etc., linked in a variety of ways, acknowledge this [6 month] anniversary.

---

[7] Student names have been changed to preserve anonymity.

As one scrolls down and delves into the past by means of these connected media streams, two stories must be told:

i. The events following the death of the young lovers, both with respect to the individuals appearing in the play, and the socio/political environment of Verona. This you get to make up as you wish.

ii. The basic events of the Romeo and Juliet story, as defined by Shakespeare, must emerge during the exploration, not in so much detail that someone entirely unacquainted with the story would understand all of its convolutions, but detailed enough so that those familiar with the play would see most of its intricacies referenced.[8]

For reference students were directed to previous projects at CDM for which Facebook was used as a vehicle for participation: (1) in a set of adventures, *The Adventures of Dapworth*, and (2) in a murder mystery, *The McLarens Murder Mystery*.[9] They were also shown different narrative models and structures in digital media that included the hypermedia novel *Califia* (transparent levels of information), various ELO sites (contemporary literary approaches), the MMORPG *Assassin's Creed II* (extensive historical setting located in Venice), and the book-to-movie *Cloud Atlas* (series of nested stories).

Choosing a Project

During the first class the students discussed the project possibilities offered. None had used social media as a narrative genre previously and a cursory discussion of story options, social media affordances, and platforms for both collaborating on the project and for the narrative itself brought about an expression of interest in trying out this new form for storytelling. Option 3, the social media narrative was chosen as the class project.

Students thought about possibilities other than *Romeo and Juliet* as the narrative. In keeping with the contemporary interest in vampire stories, one choice was Bram Stoker's novel *Dracula*. The difficulty with choosing a literary work less canonical than *Romeo and Juliet* quickly became apparent. A number of the group were international students who were not familiar with much western literature and for whom it would have been difficult to get up to speed on a complex, lengthy narrative such as *Dracula*, much less collaborate on adapting it to a new media. The story of *Romeo and Juliet* had been faithfully (and not so faithfully) reproduced in many countries so that even students who had not read the play, were familiar with the story. In addition, being a short play, adapting the story could be fitted into a 12-week class more comfortably then more complex and lengthier works.

---

[8] From the author's project archives.
[9] McLaren Murders: https://www.facebook.com/groups/183138085112157/.
Dapworth: https://www.facebook.com/groups/221561061245344/.

During the discussion about a collaborative online working space and possible options for the technology they would like to use, the students considered potential issues with copyright infringement, student confidentiality issues, and the possible need to work within a local network as a precaution against potential difficulties in these areas. The group decided to use Facebook as a space to work collaboratively while they looked into the possibility of reproducing a social media environment on the school's server[10] and created a private discussion group on the site under the name Advanced Narrative. The instructors were not invited to join this site until after the project was completed and presented. Unless students chose to share in class or via email, George and I were unaware of the behind-the-scenes process.

One of the first requirements was for everyone to read or reread the play and become familiar with the plot, the story, and the characters so that a discussion could be had on how to develop the project. A standard version was not assigned but students posted links to online resources on the group Facebook site. Among these: a free Gutenberg version of the play and a *Romeo and Juliet* family tree (Fig. 5.3). The online resources showed the heteroglossic nature of the project—this story had been adapted multiple times by each generation since its inception 500 year ago. The students could access any one of a number of versions, each of which reflected a unique interpretation of the story. The multimodal nature of the WWW ensured that the dialogue was not only about text but also about visual representations. From the get-go students referenced both text and image.

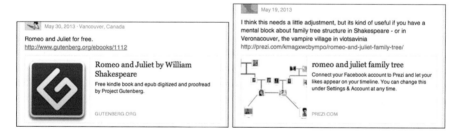

Fig. 5.3 Online resources for *Romeo and Juliet* posted to Advanced Narrative on Facebook

Discussing Theme and Media

Once the students had agreed amongst themselves on the project and finalized their choice of story, two questions were asked and discussed in class to help define the direction of both the story and the media presentation of the story.

- What was each student's main thematic interest in the *Romeo and Juliet* story?
- What social app/technology might be used to present this aspect of the story?

---

[10] The internal server solution did not work out. Students used images from the WWW in the project blogs and Facebook pages under fair use.

As a follow-up to the class discussion students were asked to write two paragraphs based on their contributions so they could clarify their ideas for the next step in the process—to work collaboratively to reach a consensus on the theme and media. Students were asked in particular to think about how their specific interest reflected the overall story and how it might be linked to the other themes fellow students had introduced during the class discussion. The complete set of students' written responses is included in Chapter 7.

The students considered the following themes:

- Love as passion
- Conflict in beliefs, culture, and lifestyle
- Communication as expression of feeling
- Social context, power, and the mercantile
- Family dynamics and communication
- External forces on Romeo and Juliet
- Transmediation and intertextuality of text

Each student brought their own perspective of why and how they would like to explore *Romeo and Juliet* through these themes, as shown in the following excerpts from their replies.

- Love is passion and with passion comes passionate decision-making, which is something we also share. That decision making based in passion that the play *Romeo and Juliet* represents, could be the beginning of a social phenomena that has replayed in circles, since the day the play became public

- I think it would be worthwhile to play with the theme of conflict in *Romeo and Juliet*. This conflict can be related to the historical age they live in, which affects their beliefs, culture, and lifestyle and it also can show up in family conflict as well. Different beliefs, culture and family situations can affect the character relationships profoundly with their families and create some conflict for them.

- I'm mostly interested in the Communication elements of Romeo and Juliet's story: but not communication as in "cell phones" or "technology" but rather communication as trying to express feelings or expectations between two people. For example: neither Juliet nor Romeo tell their parents about their relationships. Had they done so—what would have the outcome been?

- My interest in exploring and using the *Romeo and Juliet* story in a modern (social media) context is centered around the family dynamics and how communication fits into the picture. Whether it's imagining putting social media tools in the time frame that the *Romeo and Juliet* story was written or their story being played out today this story puts a spotlight on the family and how conflict gets resolved and the consequences or results of how they communicate with each other and then with the world outside.

- The main thematic interest in the story is communication. Communication is a very important skill between people and it plays a big role in each aspect of life. If we look at *Romeo and Juliet* in depth, we will find out that a big part of the sad ending is miscommunication and misunderstanding.

- My interest in Romeo and Juliet (the project) is in the transmediation of the text and the ways intertextual narratives emerge through juxtaposition of media. The old script is being replaced by the new script and the adoption rate and form is such that we can never translate all the seeding knowledge.

The media the students suggested using included the practical and the metaphoric. Following is a summary list:

- Vine (Videos/Twitter)
- Facebook
- Facebook (Tumble, Pintrest, Twitter, Wordpress)
- Digital site (thriller) with interactive mini-games that access content (emails, reports, videos)
- Blog, Tumblr, Pintrest, self-journaling and other self-reflective apps
- Wordpress and social apps such as Facebook
- Angel wings as pens used on digital paper, Twitter as mashup, Presi as map tool

Following are examples of the students' descriptions of how the technology could be used:

- A social technology to represent this could be Vine, this new app allows sharing 6 second videos using Twitter; your family is not in there, as it is on Facebook; it is fast and easy for taking and sending videos between couples. Also has the possibility for adding hash-tags to make themes spread in a community.

- Using quick interactive mini-games the spectator could hack into personal emails, discover censored reports and find hidden security footage that would reveal the lengths the government took in order to ensure that peace would prevail.

- How this echoes across time—mythological time, the time of the play, the time of its author, its time in media, its timelessness in imagination may be explored in the interlinking of diverse media forms. Twitter feeds as secret notes revealing only 140 characters of a moment, codes recoded and retweeted, appropriated and mashed into an ocean of plastic.

Stage 2 Scaffolding a Collaborative Environment

Developing a story with a cohesive plotline and interesting characters through new media that engaged the audience required listening, discussion, negotiation, and a commitment to exploring the content, the form, and the medium. Initially, George and I provided a minimum of direction as these were grad students who had all participated in successful team projects previously. The classes were structured so that lectures and presentations were during the first hour and then the class moved on to working on the project. We would participate at the beginning of the discussion to ascertain the topic for that day, and depending on the nature of the discussion, either stay and join the discussion or leave to return later for an update on progress. The first few class discussions showed us that the students enjoyed talking about ideas but were not motivated to come to conclusions about the direction for the story and weren't sure how to move the project forward. While students had an understanding of how to structure a digital media project, a literary collaboration seemed less tangible to them. George and I discussed what would be useful to direct the group. To provide direction George set a series of questions for the students to discuss so they could move the plot forward and set a deadline for a plan.

Collaborative Spaces: From Face-to-Face to Online and Back Again

Students met outside of class time to continue their discussions about the project using the Advanced Narrative Facebook site as their online collaboration space. Scheduling meetings was complicated by everyone's busy schedule and Facebook offered a way to have discussions, to post ideas, and to test out some of the artifacts they would be creating without regard for where they were or when.

As a transparent medium, Facebook made clear all of the participants' activity on the site. The site identified when and by whom posts were read and recorded conversations in sequential order. The "Seen by" feature provided a snapshot of who had opened the site, "Like" identified those who read the post and chose to acknowledge they had done so, and "Comments" provided opportunities for threaded discourse. These features provided an accurate and detailed account of discussions and activity that could be examined in light of use of the site as a space in which to collaborate. Looking at the sites "Seen by" feature showed that all students, with very few exceptions, read the posts, "Comments" showed that not all students participated through the online discussion; some students chose to wait until the class or the face-to-face (f2f) project meetings to participate in discussion.

As part of their collaborative work process students used whiteboards to enable discussion and clarify ideas. Photographs of the whiteboards were posted on the Facebook site to continue discussion and share the discussion with those who could not come to the class.

Following is part of an early Facebook exchange that addressed moving the group forward and that came to conclusions about where the story should begin (* below), how to move forward (** below), and suggested a way to deal with characters (*** below). Read the entire exchange in Chapter 7.

June 5, 2013

Sarah   Hey, Romeo and Juliet group!

         ...

         The questions are: Do the families get back together?
         Does it end with some family winning? Or still in Conflict?
         Is starting voice a specific person ... or from a choir ...
         Where are we starting from? At what point in time—and how does it end?

         ...

Nathan   Regarding the ending: A possible ending could be what is known as a "Pyrrhic Victory" Someone who wins a Pyrrhic victory has been victorious in some way; however, the heavy toll negates any sense of achievement or profit. A "Pyrrhic victory" can also mean a false or temporary victory where a win entails a loss subsequently or in the bigger picture.
         June 5, 2013 at 9:38 am · Like · 1

         ...

Ben   Conflict is something that never ends, us as humans always look for it in life.
         –   I vote for using the priest as the voice, using a religious videoblog channel on youtube. this is my reference: http://www.youtube.com/watch?v=PJvo7SB9TZY
         –   we should start from the next day they die, the first blog post could be he, being recorded while he says his good bye words, the user doesn't know who is he talking about. *Note: The story should begin here
         June 5, 2013 at 4:41 pm · Like

         ...

Carson   I vote we set up a structure, which by nature defines a set of rules, pick characters (who may be spread across time and space), and just let it evolve naturally in conversations and culture-sampling. There's no other way to write 'by committee' ... **Note: The story should evolve naturally
         June 5, 2013 at 4:45 pm · Like

         ...

Ben   Each one of us could be the perspective of a character in that case
         ***Note: A way to deal with characters
         June 5, 2013 at 4:47 pm · Like

         ...

Sarah   sounds good!
         June 5, 2013 at 4:53 pm · Like

         ... .

Facebook discussions were invariably followed by clarification and amplifica-
tion during the subsequent face-to-face (f2f) class. Students participated collaboratively in the discussion: they listened and responded, configured and reconfigured
ideas, and had to adjust their own thinking to accommodate new input. Suggestions
for plotlines, characterization, and artifacts were jotted down on whiteboards
(Fig. 5.4). Externalizing the thinking process through f2f conversations and writing
the ideas on the whiteboard gave weight to the students' contributions and provided
a sense of value for both the act of contributing and the contribution.

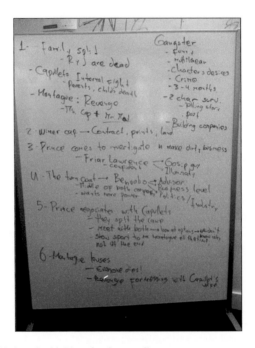

Fig. 5.4   June 6: whiteboard with ideas for the storyline

In addition to the whiteboards, which were posted on Facebook, some students
took notes that they also posted on Facebook and which provided different perspectives on the class discussions. Excerpts from Carson's notes from the June 6 class
show some of the questions that led to the ideas noted on the whiteboard and show
that students considered both the overall approach they would take and determined
specific points that would need to be investigated and/or established in developing
the story (Fig. 5.5).

What do we know?
- We have a record of Shakespeare's position.
- We know we can take different perspectives.
- Decisions have <u>consequences</u> over time.
- We can't change the <u>known</u> facts.

An option:
- Benvolio is a spy (a turncoat interested only in his own ascension to power)

Establish these points:
- We need to understand the split up of the families.
- The Capulet victory – the Prince is curious about this, leading to investigation, perhaps revealing a clue to the Prince's involvement in the deaths.
- Benvolio as turncoat.
- Prince's negotiations with the Capulets (reveal of the behind story of the Caps).
- Montague Corporation is bought out (loses).
- Final teaser. Benvolio takes over (discovers truth about Prince).[*]

Fig. 5.5 June 6: notes for storyline development posted on Facebook along with whiteboard image

The whiteboard image and the notes were posted to Facebook on the same day. Students had the opportunity to reference and compare the whiteboard (doing so would either jog their memory if they attended the class or introduce the class discussion if they hadn't) and Carson's notes in continuing their work on the project. At this point the team was exploring and tossing ideas around; there was no discussion yet about narrative coherence.

The students decided on conspiracy thriller as the genre. The story would be a vast conspiracy that involved both families, their friends, and city officials—the quest: to unravel the conspiracy. The tone of the story would be ironic with a touch of macabre humor. The story was set as an insalubrious grab for power with Benvolio conspiring with the Prince behind his friend Romeo's back to gain control of land in the City of Verona. Romeo and Juliet were, unfortunately, collateral damage. The story would uncover the land grab and show the players for what they really were. The form of the story and how it was to be unraveled was still undetermined. One suggestion from a fellow student auditing the course was shared via Facebook:

Sarah   Adam at lunch brought up an interesting idea: to frame the story using a "chorus" and have the "chorus" be news reports of the "Family Tragedy."[11]

---

[*] Facebook Advanced Narrative June 6, 2013.

[11] Facebook Advanced Narrative May 30, 2013.

Once the decisions on genre and general story line were made, the students suggested possible events that would plot the story and discussed the characters in light of these events: which characters from the original play would be necessary to the story they were creating, and which character would each of them want to represent. In a tongue-in-cheek manner they sketched out broad outlines of interaction between characters and put faces on the key players through lively descriptions. The Friar was a lascivious wretch with an eye for Juliet's nurse, who in turn, was a gossipy wench. The Prince, although power hungry, was quite a nice fellow. Lord Montague was hot-tempered. There were affairs going on, perhaps one between Lord Montague and Lady Capulet. There might even be ghosts (the dead Romeo, Juliet, and Lady Montague) and possibly a chorus.

Working together, discussing their preferences, and negotiating the roles they would take on, the students decided that the characters necessary to continuing the story would be: Benvolio (Ben), The Prince (Piper), Lord Montague and Lord Capulet (Nathan), Lady Capulet (Sarah), Friar Laurence (Carson), and the Nurse (Alexa). Tentative relationships were sketched out between the Prince and Benvolio, Friar Laurence and the Nurse, and Lord Montague and Lady Capulet. Secondary characters were Friar John (Carson), the dead Romeo, Juliet, and Lady Montague (everyone), and the Chorus.

A Disciplined Framework

The project discussions gave students a sense of value for their individual contributions and helped to build a shared purpose, but progress was slow: the group did not yet "*have a sufficiently disciplined framework to guide the project to completion.*" The students had not created a production team with defined roles for each student. Individual students were taking on tasks depending on their interest and availability. As an intervention at this point, George asked students for a plan of action, and I prompted students to create a production team similar to ones they had for other digital media projects. It was possible the students had not created a production team because the project was based in social media as a means of narrative expression. Their perception of social media may have been that it was a place for personal narrative and didn't require a production team. Social media stories were often edited collective efforts, yet the complexity of this particular assignment required the same kind of collaborative effort as did a larger production-based narrative such as a film or a video game. The group talked about the roles that would be necessary to the project from this new perspective and after discussing their talents, abilities, and interests created the following line-up of roles for the production team:

- Director: project coordinator, keeps things on track (Carson)
- Lead Writer: ensures content makes sense and is cohesive (Sarah)
- Designer: keeps site/character look/feel on track (Nathan)
- Technology: collates all social media (Piper)
- Research: provides background, context, possibility of the world (Alexa)
- Production Coordinator: ensures actual flowchart of story (Ben)

A "production team" provided the students with a framework of responsible roles necessary for a successful project. It situated the social media environment as an alternative to other media that presented stories, such as print, film, television, or games, and it set up an expectation that the "team" would work together and collaborate to complete the production of the narrative. In addition to the responsibility of creating a character that interacted with others through social media, each student now had a larger role to play and a defined responsibility for moving the project forward.

Stage 3 Building the World

Characters and Their Online Life

Carson   Did everyone get the invitation to the spreadsheet?
         EVERYTHING can be changed (including it's title).[12]

The process of unraveling a conspiracy allowed the students the opportunity to work both backward and forward in developing the story. Looking backward students could examine the original play and learn about the characters through the events that propelled the story to its unfortunate conclusion. Looking forward they could take what they'd learned about their character's traits and consider how this would affect the action of the story. The connection between the past and the future and the students' translation of this connection into the dialogue of their narrative was intertextuality made visible. The students continued to construct the story through f2f discussion. Questions asked during the previous class guided their direction in developing the story and unraveling the conspiracy through character, action, and consequence.

Carson   The Prince and Friar Laurence would have (historically) likely been inseparable.
         The way that the Prince asks questions will reveal more about the Prince, his involvement and his motivations.
         In story planning always ask, "what does this get you"—what are the consequences, advantages and problems with a plot decision?[13]

The class visualized the connections between characters and events by creating a spreadsheet on the whiteboard (Fig. 5.6). The chart they drew began at the deaths of Romeo and Juliet and progressed through actions planned for the main characters: the Prince, Benvolio, the Capulets, Montague, Friar Laurence, the Nurse, and the Chorus. An example of action was the Prince's request for proposals for a memorial plaza (first panel), meeting with the families to look at the proposals (middle panel), and awarding the contract to Benvolio, who was later killed in a dual (last panel).

---

[12] Facebook Advanced Narrative June 12, 2013.

[13] Facebook Advanced Narrative June 6, 2013.

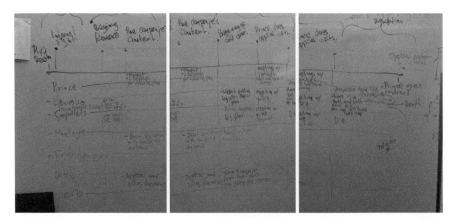

Fig. 5.6 Whiteboard data chart: preliminary character and event planning

To provide a working document that could be changed and added to, Carson had created an Excel spreadsheet based on the whiteboard planning document that the team would use as a reference point (Fig. 5.7). The chart included:

- personality traits
- primary and secondary social media
- when the character was introduced
- the first conflict
- the main conflict
- resolution
- aftermath
- primary locations
- secondary locations

With the main elements of the story clearly outlined, the students could begin to develop interactions between the characters by writing dialogue and creating text and image artifacts to substantiate the events. For instance, the Prince had asked for proposals for a memorial plaza. The request for proposal needed to be written and then mocked up on City of Verona letterhead so it could be included on the city's official website. The team made the decisions about the events together, the designer suggested the format, and the student who was the Prince would write the proposal in the prince's style.

	A	B	C	D	E	F	G
1	Characters	Personality traits	Primary Media	Secondary Media	Introduction	First conflict	
2	Linear Sequence of events				Internal fighting	Beginning Romance	The company context
3							
4	Prince	A contemplative fellow, who only sees a quiet life in his courtyard with his talking budgies.	Official web site	Wikileaks			Request for proposals for memorial plaza
5	Benvolio	Two-sided. A player. Dry two-sided humour.	Has TV sitcom gig.	Fan mail and paparazi.			Starts secret negotiations to buy all the land around the proposed plaza. Receives mysterious funding from the Freemasons.
6	Mr. Capulet	Hot tempered but fair.	Company website	Blog, email			
7	Mrs. Capulet	Passive-Aggressive; Greiving Poorly; Gossip	Facebook/ Email/ AIM		passive aggressively fighting with Mr. Capulet	Goes to speak with Mr. Montague	
8	Mr. Montague	Wise but obstinate.	Company website	Blog, email		Receives a surprise visit from Mrs. Capulet	
9	The DEAD Mrs. Montague Romeo Juliet Paris Mercutio	Dead.					
10	Friar Laurence	Has spent his life secretly making a compendium proving that most mothers are not virgins.	Reports to Rome.	Church newsletters (email; impossible to read) excrable design sense. He only has an old iPhone 3Gs: cut off from the world - cloistered metaphor.			Discussions with land owners
11	Friar John		Secret Hermetic philosopher				
12	The Nurse	Gossipy. A bit of a trollope. Has a nursing fetish.					
13	Chorus		diverse news				Official Land Title documents

Fig. 5.7 Portion of the excel data chart showing characters and events

The students had already determined the tone for the story—serious with an underlying comic/irreverent note—but there was still the matter of deciding on the look and the time and place in history in which the narrative would be set. One suggestion made was that the history be consistent with the original Shakespeare story, i.e. Verona in the 1400s, and that the era be researched for look and main events:

Carson   … I think we should set this in the 'actual' period say 1475 or thereabouts, some interesting changes of Popes at that point and ties well to the original story. We don't need to make it entirely accurate historically—just a 'flavour', a tone

There were sufficient resources on the web to create a Renaissance Verona; an issue, however, that might require addressing was how to incorporate contemporary media into a Renaissance story and still maintain authenticity. To authors accustomed to creating for print or for film it might be a profound challenge to create a coherent narrative from a collage-like presentation of images, text, and media from different eras. To a new generation accustomed to the mashups intrinsic to the internet, however, the plausibility of bringing together images and media from different eras wasn't an issue. Suspension of disbelief was more an unconscious than a conscious act. What might have appeared as an inconsistency to an audience a number of years ago, i.e. using Facebook in fourteenth century Verona, became, instead, part of the intertextual collage that was being created and that bridged the centuries.

Character Development

Once the story line was determined and the characters were chosen, each student was charged with creating their character and choosing the social media channels that best revealed their character's personality through behavior rather than description. Nuances could be shown through the way a character used text, image, or a particular medium to interface with other characters and to share their story.

Carson   … we do have an immediate assignment already (which involves actually skimming the play at least for character data). I want everyone to do that, as well as the short character bio, Facebook pages for individual characters; then we've got a basis to stand on … .
June 21, 2013 at 11:14 am · Like
         …

Ben   a OK, so lets do this, each one of us create the character bio, and then we can meet Monday 5 p.m. with that info. Are we gonna use Facebook or the CDM social for those character profiles?

June 21, 2013 at 11:17 am · Like
         …

Carson   Try Facebook for character profiles I think. You'll need some bogus google email or something to make another account.

   Facebook provided a framework of predetermined categories that revealed a person's likes and interests, like a paint-by-number portrait that just needed filling in. In addition to the textual dialogue possibilities, Facebook offered the students space for photos, events, interests, and lists of friends, in addition to a timeline of events for constructing their character. The ease with which students could search and copy images from other sites was an advantage when creating individual characters. Rather than beginning with a blank slate, students could pick images of individuals who they felt were representative of the persona they wanted to create, and build on an existing media presence/image.

   The first character created and posted on Facebook was Lady Capulet. The image used for the profile was of a contemporary actress. As the first bio, the image set an example from which the other students took their cue. The remaining characters are also shown as contemporary individuals in contemporary environments. The Facebook page was mocked up in Photoshop and used as the format for all the Facebook profile/posts.

Sarah   … I'll just mock up the Facebook profile/ posts all in Photoshop—when the time comes to add text, that is

Shakespeare's characters are popular on Facebook and there are numerous Lady Capulet and Lord Montague sites. Would this create a problem for readers who were searching for this particular story to become friends and join the group? Carson suggested that if sufficient information is provided to ensure that the members can recognize each other, there should be no problem with the surfeit of similar characters.

After the initial discussion about each character's personality, the students created their characters with little further input from the team and posted the completed Facebook pages on the Advanced Narrative site. Each page revealed the character's personality: Valentino (Lord) Capulet's character was emphasized through images of expensive toys such as his Ferrari, Friar Laurence's penchant for philosophizing was revealed in posts that include a link to an application that kept track of sins (Fig. 5.8). URLs for the different Facebook pages are noted at the end of Chapter 6.

Fig. 5.8 Friar Laurence shows a penchant for philosophizing

Facebook facilitated the growth of a collaborative culture as students used the site to advantage to discuss and work through ideas. Fellow students responded, were supportive, and provided input. Students used the group page to share their ambivalence, discuss ideas, and come to conclusions about how to present a personality. The Nurse, a minor figure, was intended to add a lighter, comedic, and sexy note. The following Facebook discussion looks at the question of how broad to draw her character and whether to use a well-known personality's photo to emphasize these characteristics. The discussion also makes the important observation that how the character is portrayed will influence "the nature of her relationships."

Carson   Nice—two nurses the second one looks like even more trouble than the first lol
           July 8, 2013 at 10:34 pm · Like · 1
Alexa   Hehehe great! She looks a bit naughty and playful. She is older than the other one. She's fat so she enjoys eating food!
           July 8, 2013 at 10:36 pm · Like
Carson   lol just a 'bit'—perfect! Maybe we can keep the first one as a story about the one that got fired—funny!
           July 8, 2013 at 10:38 pm · Like · 1
Alexa   May be so this actress would be perfect, too.
           July 8, 2013 at 10:42 pm · Like
           …
Alexa   That's true. I feel much comfortable with this actress as a nurse. I don't know how to define beauty in people's eyes!
           July 8, 2013 at 10:52 pm · Like
Carson   Nobody does
           July 8, 2013 at 10:59 pm · Like · 1
Alexa   Absolutely right! … He gave me clues "mid 30s", "fat" and it's ok if she's blonde.
           July 8, 2013 at 11:06 pm · Like
Carson   He sees either as an option. If she's young sexy and beautiful it influences the internal dynamic differently than old and 'in the family'. It can be either, and like I said we can even refer to the other one we don't use, but it has to be 'logical'—the nature of the character influences the nature of her relationships.
           July 9, 2013 at 12:32 am · Like

Connecting Characters

All the characters now had personal profiles on Facebook. As time strode implacably forward it became apparent to the team that they needed a schedule to address items necessary to the story's progress, such as each character's posts and personal interactions (Fig. 5.9). The number of posts for each character was set at eight; these were to describe events, set a mood, or be correspondence with another character.

Fig. 5.9 The schedule set requirements for each character's interactions

Each student needed to consider which media would be best for individual posts — video, photo, audio, text — and which platform would best suit their character — blog, Twitter, YouTube. Students also needed to confer with each other to plan out the network of conversations and actions that went on between their characters and to write and create the artifacts in tandem. Google Docs was chosen as the repository to house the narrative artifacts and students began to build up a repertoire of dialogues, posts, or journal entries for their characters. Figure 5.10 shows Google's *Welcome to Google Docs* and the first upload, the draft versions of Lady Capulet's personal blog.

to share on facebook (instead of just google hangouts) the link to the shared proto-document

https://docs.google.com/.../1jSz467BUR-NXhC8UypfbA_Jv8Qh.../edit

Welcome to Google Docs

ACCOUNTS.GOOGLE.COM

Fig. 5.10 *Welcome to Google Docs* post on Facebook links to content written for Lady Capulet in the newly created Google Docs repository*

---

*Facebook Advanced Narrative post by Sarah July 21, 2013.

Figure 5.11 shows the content of Lady Capulet's Draft Script that is shared with the team in Google Docs. Figure 5.12 shows the completed entry in the blog *Lady Capulet Speaks*. This first blog post sets the scene for Lady Capulet's future actions and begins to build her character for us by providing a glimpse into her point of view about family, duty, and love. The blog is very personal and over time reveals her sorrow over her husband's murder, her views on Benvolio and on Lord Montague, and her deep (business) involvement with the Prince. Each of the posts reveals something about the conspiracy from her perspective. The Draft Script contains many more items than are posted in the official blog. Photos, reminisces, notes on meetings, and other reveals are jotted down for potential use.

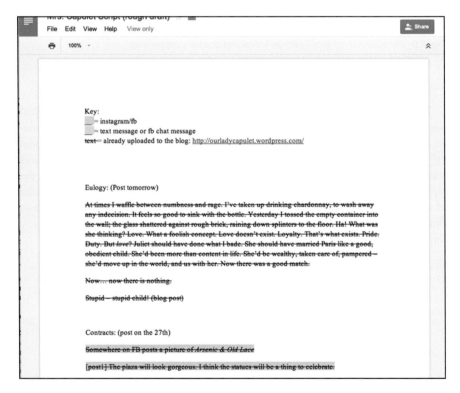

Fig. 5.11 Google Docs: Lady Capulet's Script (rough draft)

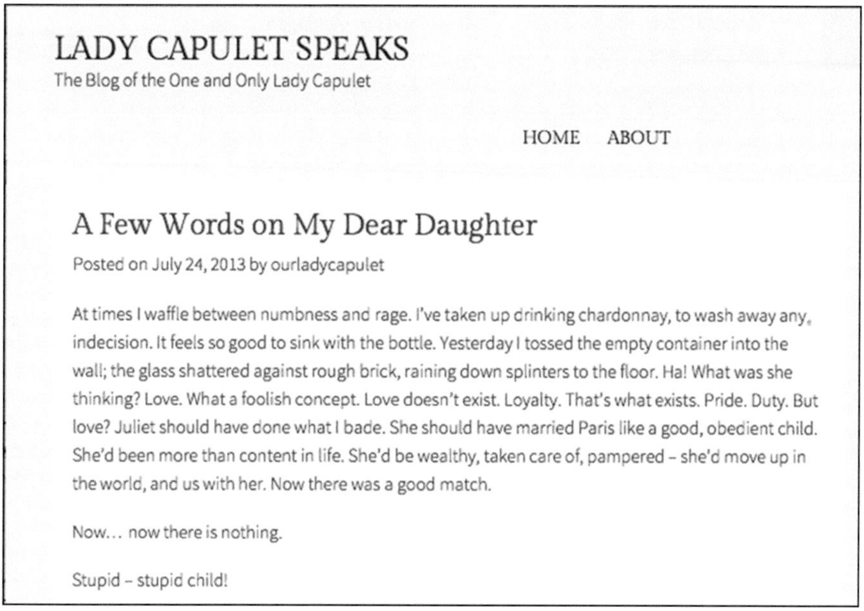

LADY CAPULET SPEAKS
The Blog of the One and Only Lady Capulet

                                                              HOME   ABOUT

A Few Words on My Dear Daughter
Posted on July 24, 2013 by ourladycapulet

At times I waffle between numbness and rage. I've taken up drinking chardonnay, to wash away any indecision. It feels so good to sink with the bottle. Yesterday I tossed the empty container into the wall; the glass shattered against rough brick, raining down splinters to the floor. Ha! What was she thinking? Love. What a foolish concept. Love doesn't exist. Loyalty. That's what exists. Pride. Duty. But love? Juliet should have done what I bade. She should have married Paris like a good, obedient child. She'd been more than content in life. She'd be wealthy, taken care of, pampered – she'd move up in the world, and us with her. Now there was a good match.

Now… now there is nothing.

Stupid – stupid child!

Fig. 5.12 Lady Capulet's personal blog at https://ourladycapulet.wordpress.com

Lady Capulet's scripts included both monologues and dialogues. Input from co-participants was needed to complete the dialogues and comments were welcomed from the entire team, as noted in the following Facebook comment. Figure 5.13 shows the dialogue as it was written by Sarah and filled in by Nathan.

Sarah   Lady Capulet's fb convos with Mr. Montague & Mr. Capulet
         (please note that the male parts have not been filled in as that will be
         Michael's job smile emoticon)
         https://docs.google.com/.../1AldM7xXR7lSDokmjekJRc9P142l.../edit
         and I can correct her conversation to match Mr. Montague's & Mr. Capulet if
         you feel so inspired.[14]

---

[14] Facebook Advanced Narrative posted by Sarah July 23, 2013.

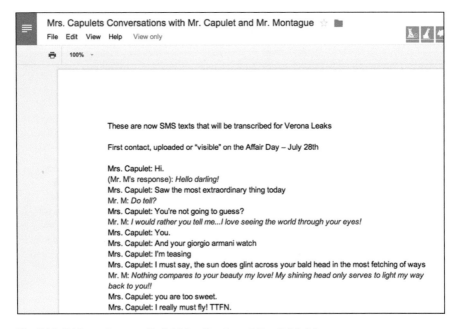

Fig. 5.13 Dialogue between (Lady) Mrs. Capulet and (Lord) Mr. Montague

Each student chose to reveal their character in different ways. The Friar kept a number of different websites, each of which revealed a different aspect of his personality. His interest in the nurse is revealed in a page from his diary which includes his drawings, shown in Fig. 5.14.

Fig. 5.14 Friar Laurence's secret life disclosed in a page of his personal diary

As the network of narrative artifacts increased, the group looked at ways to provide paths into the story. The *City of Verona Speaks* site was created to represent the official voice of The Prince, share the city administrative activities, and act as a portal to each character's personal Facebook page.

Sarah   Okay, I've done some (minor) overhaul of the Verona homepage—so that it becomes a hub/ landing page ...

I've also added all the links to the menu header, linking to our Facebooks and blogs ...

This way there will be a chorus of sorts opening and leading and directing the viewer to the narrative hubs.

The student's created the site on the university server as a facsimile Facebook page as they thought at the time that it might be possible to create the entire project on the private network. This did not prove possible. Links to Facebook character profiles took readers off the university site. Nevertheless the site remained on the proprietary network as there was no time to port it to Facebook. Figure 5.15a shows the site masthead and Fig. 5.15b shows the invitation to a discussion forum concerning a proposal for a memorial to Romeo and Juliet.

Fig. 5.15 (**a**) The City of Verona official website. (**b**) An invitation to a discussion forum on a Romeo and Juliet memorial

Stage 4 Revealing the Conspiracy

WikiLeaks Metaphor

As of yet there was no way to expose the conspiracy. On the surface, Romeo and Juliet's deaths were not suspicious, only tragic—an inciting incident/action was required to begin the investigation. The group decided to create a secret organization of concerned citizens with a mission to find out the truth about dubious activities undertaken by city administrators over the Romeo and Juliet memorial. In response, the city would also investigate.

Sarah   … I think that could be a wiki-leak-esque website. A conspiracy theorist site …
            And the City of Verona could post the scandal (scandal of the utmost! this
            wiki-leaks blog has outted the affair!) and the characters could respond (those
            who have access to the annoying bill site/ main hub). This ties the whole thing
            together. The Main Hub is the place where everything is aired to the public.
            Problem solved.[15]

Using the *WikiLeaks* metaphor students created a *Verona Leaks* site that shared information about citizens' ongoing investigations into city administrators. To steer readers to the site, the students had concerned citizens hack the *City of Verona Speaks* site, warn the citizens of Verona that they are being lied to, and point them to *Verona Leaks* for elucidation (Fig. 5.16).

Fig. 5.16 Hackers from *Verona Leaks* post a warning on the *City of Verona* site

Students adapted the *WikiLeaks* logo to the new citizen's site, leaving the top part of the hourglass empty, substituting Italy for the world in the bottom section, replacing *WikiLeaks* with *VeronaLeaks*, and changing the color. The mission of the site was clearly stated on the portal page (Fig. 5.17):

To uncover the lies and secrets being held from our Verona Citizens. To Speak the Absolute Truth. To Show the Facts and bring awareness to Verona. Verona Leaks is a non-for-profit organization, ferreting out all information withheld from public view. The goal is simple, if knowledge is power, then give the citizens back their power.

---

[15] Facebook Advanced Narrative July 25, 2013.

Fig. 5.17 A new citizen's organization, *Verona Leaks*, was set up with a mission to investigate City of Verona activities

The site was set up so that basic information about an investigation was provided in a short post and this was followed by links to documentary evidence. The first post was related to the proposal to build a commemorative statue for Romeo and Juliet. Emails had been found between Lord Capulet and the Prince and between Lord Montague and the Prince that suggested collusion in how the contract for the memorial was awarded (Fig. 5.18).

After the untimely death of the Capulet and Montague progeny, a court investigation was launched. As quickly as the case was opened it was closed. By the following week (June 05, 20xx) the court ruled the deaths as suicide and no reparation was plausible. The two respective families stated in the *Verona Sun*:

"We plan on building bridges where our children have been buried. The town square will have a statue in their commemoration."

As of Wednesday this afternoon, **Mr. Valentino Capulet** was seen having tea with the **Prince** as reported by *The People's Magazine*. Though the magazine went no further in speculation, emails between the two have revealed contracting plans for the town square, and a sizeable donation on part of the Prince. These monetary transactions fund the enterprises of the Capulet's Firm, and their other questionably legal activities. **Mr. Salvatore Montague** was also seen in the company of the **Prince**, and the following emails suggest further transactions.

Emails

Mr. Valentino Capulet to the Prince	Emails [link]
.	.
Mr. Salvatore Montague to the Prince	Emails [link]

Reported July 27, 20xx

Fig. 5.18 *Verona Leaks* post connecting Romeo and Juliet's death to current scandalous affairs in Verona

The following posts revealed more corruption and identified which officials were involved in activities that were either blatant grabs for power and money or constituted immoral activities. The site bristled with authentic documents the students had created to substantiate *Verona Leaks* findings: official documents, fabricated emails, letters, and Facebook chats, and scanned handwritten journals. Figures 5.19 and 5.20 are representative of these artifacts.

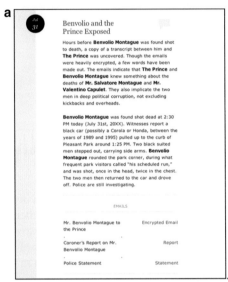

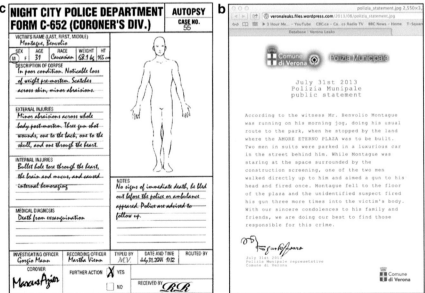

Fig. 5.19 (**a**) Blog page exposing Benvolio and the Prince and linked documentary evidence: (**b**) Coroner's Report (**c**) Police Statement

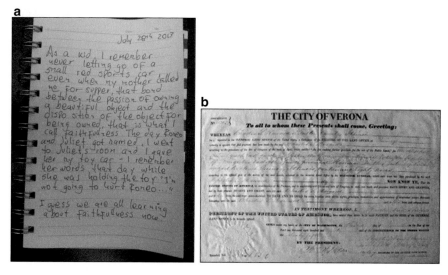

Fig. 5.20 Documentary evidence: (**a**) page from Benvolio's personal journal (**b**) City of Verona land grant document

Students continued to collaborate on creating documentation and provide assistance to each other as the documentation for individual artifacts and for connected artifacts such as conversations increased in number with the evolving story.

Ben   Hello guys, do you wanna meet today or tomorrow for taking a look at how are you going with the posts and to see how can we help each other?

But ensuring that documentation was date sequenced correctly and that posts reflected accurately what events had occurred was time consuming and occasionally frustrating. The following exchange notes in particular that once a character is (really) dead, posts from him should not appear; it also reflects the good naturedness of the exchanges.

Carson   Please note: the dead tell no tales. therefore any 'back dating' of conversations is temporally illogical. If such documents need to be produced they will have to be reproductions of other media, emails uncovered and scans from paper documents.
         Seen by 9
Sarah   on that note, Alan, Benvolio should be dead by now. I'm correcting the coroner's report so that it reflects the time (so that you're not posting from the dead) but just … no more posts from poor Benny. If you want him to speak from the dead, he's going to need extraneous documentation (journal entries, emails, things that can be found days later by snoops and posted on 3rd party sites)
         July 31, 2013 at 2:09 pm · Like

Carson   yes i noticed that too ..the only other option as to suggest he's not dead but gone into hiding and faked it/… . but lets just kill the little bastard
July 31, 2013 at 2:54 pm · Like

Sarah   I have him killed by 3 bullet wounds … but he died of bleeding out from the wounds, not immediately. The time of death is stated at 2:30 pm smile emoticon
July 31, 2013 at 2:56 pm · Like

Carson   Oh juicey. Wish we had time for the graphics.
July 31, 2013 at 2:57 pm · Like

Sarah   The best I got was a fake coroner's report. Thank goodness for photoshop
July 31, 2013 at 2:57 pm · Like

Carson   wink emoticon
July 31, 2013 at 2:58 pm · Like

The Gumshoe Wraps Up

The students now had two important "hubs" for their narrative: *The City of Verona Speaks* site, which provided the official version of events, and the *Verona Leaks* site, which revealed what was happening behind the scenes. They were spending considerable time creating text and image artifacts, ensuring connections between characters made sense, and providing for continuity between conversations. The narrative had two main entry points into a network of characters and events but did not yet provide a compelling experience of story: what strategies related to the construction of the narrative could they use to engage their audience in a suspenseful directed path rather than a random exploration of interesting artifacts?

When the *Verona Leaks* site was set up, one of the follow-up ideas was that the city would hire an external investigator as a response to citizens' concerns. An external investigation would provide an opportunity for an impartial, third person narrator, without a point of view, who could reliably present unbiased evidence. In effect, this would be the "frame" or chorus that had been suggested at the start of the project. Through the process of creation the story had migrated from thriller to detective genre. The structure of a detective story offered a way into the network of information that was direct and uncomplicated. Students could lay their network out before the audience in a genre that was familiar to most people.

The students created the law/detective firm of J. Murphy & Sons whose investigation would provide a method for presenting the Verona/Romeo and Juliet story. They created a company website to establish credibility and provide a semblance of substance for the data that would be presented. Using a traditional detective story technique, students began the story with the lead investigator, Mr. J. Murphy, summarizing why the company had been hired. "A Letter to the Council" (reproduced in total in the next section) clarified that the firm had been hired by the City of Verona to investigate the site *Verona Leaks* as well as recent "unsettling" events in the city, including the deaths of Romeo and Juliet. The letter became the portal to the story: it led the council to documentary evidence through links to the two main information "conduits," the sites *City of Verona Speaks* and *Verona Leaks*. Referring and linking to these sites provided for the two differing points of view into the story, the official view of events on the *City of Verona Speaks* site, and the people's view on the *Verona Leaks* site. The juxtaposition of the two nicely reflected Bakhtin's heterglossic opposing centrifugal and centripetal forces that continually modify the use of language and media within a cultural context. Students left the story open to continuing investigation: the presentation J. Murphy made was of "… evidence accumulated *so far* in the course of the *preliminary* investigation … ." which might yet reveal new information and change the direction of the story.

As additional media, a QR code was added to provide for quick mobile phone access to the documentation. The final J. Murphy website the students posted included the Letter to the Council (Fig. 5.21), an Investigation Chart of Character Relationships (Fig. 5.22), and an Investigators Chart of Current Characters Media ports (Fig. 5.23). The firm noted that the site was private and required an invitation to view (Fig. 5.24).

Fig. 5.21 J. Murphy & Sons LLP website and QR code

J. Murphy's Investigation Chart of Character Relationships was a rudimentary diagram of the firm's investigation; it identified websites and characters and implied connections through juxtaposition and linking. The chart showed that J. Murphy investigated *Verona Leaks*, followed this up with an investigation of the City's site, and then went on to investigate private citizens. The chart included, among other entries, the Royal Baby, confirmation of the relationship between The Prince and Lady Capulet (both the baby and the dotted line), and the Black Mask site, a mysterious site that may have been set up by the deep throat of *Verona Leaks* revelations.

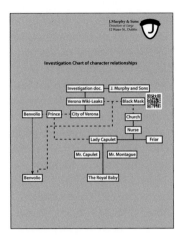

Fig. 5.22 J. Murphy's Chart of Character Relationships

In its investigation, the students had J. Murphy track the Social Media that characters used. This type of media-linking information is shown on many personal and commercial websites, and in those cases, allows the viewer to link to the sites specified. Verona's council, which didn't appear on the relationships chart, was included here. The chart showed that all the characters and organizations used email, Facebook, Wordpress, Twitter, and an RRS feed, and that in addition the J. Murphy and Black Mask sites used QR codes.

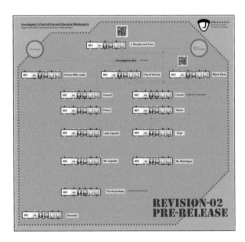

Fig. 5.23 J. Murphy's Analysis of Character Media Ports

Fig. 5.24 The J. Murphy site required an invitation to view

The J. Murphy site provided the frame the story needed to be presented cohesively rather than as a loose assemblage of characters and events. With the deadline upon them the group decided to present their story to their instructors in context as a performance: J. Murphy and Sons reported to the City of Verona's Council on their progress in the investigation.

Ladies and Gentleman: After Love Comes Destruction

The morning meeting was in session: The first order of business was for J. Murphy to introduce the company to the Council and to present an overview of the project by sharing the *Letter to the Council*.

> Letter to the Council
>
> To Whom it May Concern,
>
> Good afternoon, Ladies and Gentlemen, Members of the City Council of Verona, Justice of the Peace Madame Borgia, and Presiding Council Head Georgio Johnsoni. My name is Paddy Murphy, representative of Jesus Murphy and Sons LLP in Dublin, Ireland. J. Murphy and Sons have been contracted by the City Council of Verona as an outside law firm with extensive experience in complex snafu litigation, in order to conduct an impartial investigation into recent events in Verona.
>
> J. Murphy and Sons were initially hired to investigate the claim that a hacker organization known as Verona Leaks had begun infiltrating the City of Verona Speaks website in order to, it was further claimed, deceitfully manipulate funding invested in a City of Verona re-building campaign. This campaign was about to be initiated through an open bid, with a competition to design, build, and install a public sculptural project, The Plaza del Amore Eterno.
>
> Shortly after beginning this investigation we were further contracted by the City to investigate the circumstances behind the recent tragic deaths in the Capulet and Montague Families, the very families the Plaza project sought to honor. Starting from a maze of interconnections discovered in documents obtained from the Police connected with the double suicide of Romeo Montague and Juliet Capulet, we have further delved into the apparent murders of Valentino Capulet, Salvatore Montague, and Benvolio Montague.

We present to you this afternoon, documents that reveal far reaching connections in the Verona Leaks case, documents suggesting that the sources of funding and motivations of those providing them may be linked in ways that have serious consequences for the City of Verona.

The investigation reveals three primary conduits of information playing throughout the web of interconnections rapidly being built by the various stakeholders in these contract negotiations. They are:

The City of Verona Speaks web site http://bp.gnwc.private
Verona Leaks http://veronaleaks.wordpress.com
The Black Mask http://cosmoschaosandthemask.wordpress.com

Persons of interest and current suspects in the case may or may not be linked through to from these sources. Some information exists only as screenshots and scans obtained under covert surveillance and will therefore exist in the database only, as digital documents.

So without further ado our detectives will present to the Council the evidence accumulated so far in the course of the preliminary investigation, starting with portfolio analyses of each character and the situations those characters seem to be involved with.

We sincerely express our desire that the further investigation of these matters be addressed in ways directed by the Council, and thereby await your decision as to which further directions may—or may not—be pursued in relation to certain 'uncomfortable facts' these preliminary findings suggest.

Yours with all due respect,

J. Murphy

Once J. Murphy (performed by Carson) had provided a summary and clarified the company's role as investigators, the students continued to present the documentary evidence they had uncovered in the course of their investigation. Each student provided support to the presentation by introducing their own character. The documentation of the different media forms the characters used such as email and blogs showed the conventions of these forms were well understood by the students.

In their short presentation the students were able to show the complexity of the narrative with its multi-level plot, many paths, and substantial number of narrative artifacts that supported the characters and events. The students indicated at the end of the presentation that they had difficulty coming to terms with how a social media narrative could be structured as a story and presented to an audience. This was substantiated by comments posted on Facebook just a few days previously:

Ben   Also, it is good to take a look at the whole content in the pages, and to see if we need to add, move, clarify stuff. So the story is clear
       July 30, 2013 at 4:07 pm · Like

Carson   Yes..so the template is clear anyway. We shouldn't even pretend that this is a 'story'. To have a story means people actually have to talk to each other—play the part(s). It's pretty interesting as a framework for an emergent transmedia piece however, but not even so much for the 'plot' it only marginally has, but for the way it plays out as interactive narrative generating emergent forms that are barely even beginning to show and to which people's involvement (or lack thereof) are entirely and appropriately embodied in the narrative. So it's a framework experiment. One that _could_ lead to a story, but not by Thursday. I stand with it as a _very_ interesting set of interactive game rules, a story mechanic. That's the only way it makes sense to present it.
          July 31, 2013 at 1:30 am · Like

Carson   That, and a discussion and identification of problems experienced _with the media_ not the players …
          July 31, 2013 at 1:33 am · Like

The project was both about producing a narrative and about the collaborative process required to do so. The strength of collaboration is not only in the final narrative artifact produced but also in the support members give each other in the various activities they must undertake, from planning to production to presentation. From a perspective of collaboration, the team's final presentation showed an understanding of the requirement for both individuals to present independent views and for the group to work together to present a collective view. It isn't always necessary to agree. It is always necessary to support the group in moving forward.

Afterstory

Carson   I'm thinking we could open this group to George and Krystina now as part of the final documentation … any votes?

After the presentation the students provided extra details about the process and the documentation repositories. Figure 5.25 shows images from Facebook and "Faked" documentation on Google Docs.

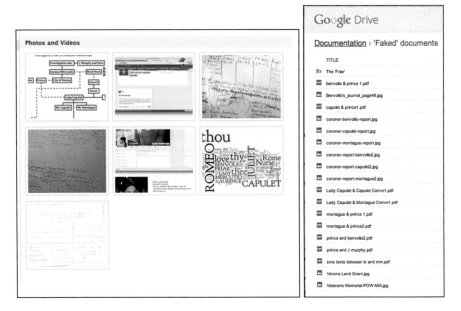

Fig. 5.25 Facebook and Google Docs repositories

The instructors, as mentioned earlier, were not privy to the students' Facebook working site and much of the process of creating the narrative had been hidden while in progress. The instructors were exposed to the external actions of the students' collaboration until the site was shared, and revealed the machinations behind the work. The discussions on the site would be invaluable in gaining insight into the students' experience. Students were also set the following questions to generate discussion about the process and project from their perspective:

- What did you learn from the project?
- What worked, what didn't, and why?
- What would you change in the design/production of the project?
- How well or badly did the team work together, generally and individually (no need to detail each individual)?

The next chapter provides a summary of the students' responses to these questions. It begins with a brief assessment of what the project achieved from my perspective.

Chapter 6
Collaborative Authoring in a Social Media World

Summary

Narrative interaction is driven by agency, dialogism, and collaboration that together with the material presence of content, form, and medium constitute the narrative experience. The first section of this book provides examples of different levels of collaboration that interactive narrative has offered people over the centuries. It shows that digital interactive narrative followed interactive print in providing readers opportunities for manipulating characters and events and determining direction through a story. The narrative experience has been shaped by the mechanics (analog or digital) that delineate the interaction between people and narrative content, whether as author or as reader or both.

What, in summary, is the result of the project *Romeo and Juliet on Facebook: After Love Comes Destruction*?

> *When reiterated through the lens of critical analysis the resulting interactive narrative demonstrates that a social media environment can facilitate a meaningful and productive collaborative authorial experience with an end interactive narrative that has an abundance of networked, personally expressive, visually and textually referential content.*

There are two aspects of the project that are most meaningful for my continuing study of "the word in living conversation." The first is the fashioning of a collaborative culture and environment for authoring and the second is the use of social media affordances for the construction of an interactive story. The point of the project was to have a group of people engage in the creation of a complex, multi-layered, multimodal narrative that was as messy and convoluted as real life (or more so). The people in the group were both author and reader and it was irrelevant if there were no future readers as the point of the narrative experience was to offer this small group the pleasure and entertainment of authoring using social media.

© The Author(s) 2016
K. Madej, *Interactivity, Collaboration, and Authoring in Social Media*,
International Series on Computer Entertainment and Media Technology,
DOI 10.1007/978-3-319-25952-9_6

Collaboration is not for everyone as creating a collaborative culture requires a certain level of attention from participants. It helps if they can:

- define and build a shared purpose
- make a combined effort to reach that purpose
- create an environment that allows each one to work flexibly so they can add their own nuances to the project
- have a sufficiently disciplined framework to guide the project to completion
- cultivate an ethic of contribution
- view collaboration as valued
- appropriately reward collaboration

Students responded to the need for collaboration to differing degrees. Students' comments indicated that enthusiasm at the beginning of the project ensured everyone was involved. As the project progressed, demands on individual's time from other projects meant that not everyone was as committed to dedicating the hours required for collaboration. Developing individual characters was easy. Creating a consistent tone across characters was more difficult. Ensuring the conversations between characters both maintained tone and carried the story forward was the most difficult. The opportunities for collaboration in this project existed particularly in the conversations between characters. This tandem, dual way of working was new and a challenge which some students were able to meet better than others, possibly more because of effort than skill. Being a skillful writer facilitated the process and in the comments one of the students noted that the course description should have indicated that writing was a large component of the course.

Using social media as an extension of the content rather than simply as a mediator of content requires exploiting regularly used communication skills within storytelling. It works best if the author is completely familiar and comfortable with the media used. When writers use words, sentences and paragraphs to create their story they don't have to think about how these will look as text (either print or digital). While a new generation of readers has grown up using social media as a function of their daily life and has integrated these tools as part of their communication vocabulary, as Cooper found out when he introduced his students to *Hypertext Hotel*, it sometimes takes a while to learn to use these tools to tell a story. This was the case for *Romeo and Juliet on Facebook*. The traditional routes to creating a story—building character, setting, storyline, plot and creating atmosphere—were each individually manageable. This was content. The difficulty came in how to use the nature of social media to effect in the story and then how to use the medium itself as a platform of presentation. The story artifacts created took advantage of a limited number of social media forms: email, blogs, Facebook—but this cadre of tools was extended with interesting documentary evidence such as journals and medical reports. The students learned from the difficulties they encountered in creating a story in this new environment. As Carson pointed out, repeated here because of its importance, what students had was a new story mechanic in which people performed parts, but they hadn't quite got to completing the story.

Carson   … It's pretty interesting as a framework for an emergent transmedia piece
           however, but not even so much for the 'plot' it only marginally has, but for the
           way it plays out as interactive narrative generating emergent forms that are
           barely even beginning to show and to which people's involvement (or lack
           thereof) are entirely and appropriately embodied in the narrative. So it's a
           framework experiment… a _very_ interesting set of interactive game rules, a
           story mechanic.

This was particularly evident in the final presentation. While the story was not
intended for a large audience, rather a small, bookclub type audience, it was intended
for use online. This implied a requirement for posting it somewhere, somehow, so
that others (even in a limited group) were aware of the story and could access it.
J. Murphy needed that elusive online launch point. Few of us would not recognize
the night before conversation:

Carson   The night before the final presentation: what are we going to talk about?…we
           should have an agenda; perhaps people can post items for discussion here
           then.
           July 30, 2013 at 3:47 pm · Like
Sarah   … we should have at least an idea *of* a presentation yet alone a POWERPOINT
           July 30, 2013 at 3:56 pm · Edited · Like

Student Perspective

Overall the students felt they had learned a considerable amount about collaborating
on the production of a social media story. All of them had suggestions for how to
make the project better; they enjoyed the project even if they might not want to do
it again:

> I really liked the final result, I think it is a nice prototype or first iteration of
> something that could be amazing. (Ben)

> As much as I enjoyed working on this project, and I really did, I would not do
> it again. (Sarah)

Following is a summary of responses to the questions asked at the end of the
presentation.

- What did you learn from the project?

  Students learned about storytelling, social media, and collaboration.

  Students learned about different elements of story telling. They learned how to
  create a character through social media, communicate the character to others,
  and to connect characters to each other. Thinking in their own character's shoes
  helped determine the best media to represent them. Connecting characters

required knowledge about each other's characters and a commitment to accommodating different styles of communication.

Students experimented with new media platforms and learned how to use social media. They learned that scripting in advance makes uploading easier; that backdating is difficult so planning is important; that repositories can be organized to support plot points.

Students learned that the media can act as part of the story. They learned that the interactions between characters naturally developed within the medium and added depth to the character and the relationship.

- What worked, what didn't, and why?

   Students felt what worked well was creating a database of artifacts and events. They found they could use Facebook for individual character profiles and Wordpress for the main story as the blog platform allowed back-dating without anyone being the wiser.

   Students felt it was useful to have instructors as part of the process to help direct efforts to the more important parts of producing a narrative such as developing a storyline.

   Students appreciated a lead writer to learn from, and having the lead writer provide a first example (Lady Montague draft).

   Students felt what didn't work was using an in-house Facebook facsimile for the main Town of Verona site, as the technical difficulties ate up time.

   Scheduling was also a difficulty as the amount of time required to create a network of conversations/actions was underestimated. Students felt that with better time management a tighter, more cohesive structure for the story would have been achieved.

- What would you change in the design/production of the project?

   Student's felt the production team should be a required part of the project and each role in the production team should be made clear. Students need to be prepared for a lot of writing.

   Students thought integrating the narrative theory taught in the class would benefit the development of the narrative as would hearing about the experience of being a digital media writer from someone in the industry.

   Students thought a public demonstration requirement would provide more motivation for creating a deliverable product.

- How well or badly did the team work together, generally, and individually (no need to detail each individual)?

   Students thought the team as a unit worked well, particularly in f2f meetings. Initially team members contributed equally. Final production was largely left to only two-three students.

Students thought communications was occasionally an issue as individuals who needed it could have asked for assistance in a more timely fashion.

Students felt time management became difficult because of occasional late delivery of some aspect of the project. Sometimes this difficulty arose because of technology problems such as team members using different platforms for their characters.

Reiteration

The project successfully provided an opportunity for students to collaborate on producing a narrative in a new form yet in a medium that was familiar and common to all them. It demonstrated advantages and disadvantages with the type of team created, the kind of collaboration required, the story used, and the use of social media. While movies and games require teams, writing is usually a function of the lead writer and his/her team of writers. With the *Romeo and Juliet* project everyone was on the spot to create characters and settings, to collaborate in producing a story and plot, "and to integrate their perspective with the shifting directions that emerged in the group process."[1] The project engaged the students in aspects of story development that took them beyond both the print or game concerns they were familiar with. Students' personal experience with social media allowed them to be intrigued rather than frightened off by trying out a new genre.

The main difficulty that I saw for the students was that not all of them had enough knowledge/experience of/with writing and producing narratives in any form to work in a new form so that much of the responsibility landed on the shoulders of just a few students. The second issue was lack of understanding or appreciation for team/collaboration dynamics. To mitigate these issue, the subsequent iteration of the project at Georgia Tech was planned to include activities that provided students with experience in the development of storyline, characters, and setting in more traditional settings before they tackled these elements in a social media environment. As Sarah said in one of her comments: "scripting almost everything in advance made uploading and transmitting the media all that much easier."[2] Simple techniques make it easier to complete the production of the narrative successfully, but only if one is aware of them before hand. Another planned addition to the subsequent project was team-building to familiarize students with the value of sharing, discussing, and negotiating as part and parcel of the collaboration process. Using a revised syllabus, the project was reiterated in an undergraduate Narrative Across Media course in the Spring 2014 term at Georgia Tech. The larger class of 17 students provided an opportunity to create four teams, each of which tackled a different story. The four stories were: *Around the World in Eighty Days, Dracula, The Great Gatsby,* and

---

[1] Personal correspondence from Brett Pawson, June 24, 2015.
[2] Email August 1, 2013.

Where'd You Go Bernadette. The students had 8 weeks to work on the final product but there were many activities in the 6 earlier weeks of the course that provided students with experience in creating storylines, characters, and settings. A future article is planned to show how changes in formatting the project for the students affected the development of the story and the collaboration process.

Access to Sites

The Indefatigable J. Murphy & Sons' Website, the website of the firm of investigators hired by the City of Verona to look into organizational leaks and the deaths of Romeo and Juliet, provides information crucial to understanding the events that occurred.

At https://jmurphyandsons.wordpress.com

The City of Verona Speaks, the official city website, links readers to the individual Facebook sites of the main players.

At http://projects.gnwc.ca/bp/

Personal profiles linked to the main *City of Verona Speaks* site and on Facebook:

https://www.facebook.com/prince.escalus.3158

https://www.facebook.com/benvolio.montague.921677

https://www.facebook.com/salvatore.montague?ref=pymk&fref=pymk

https://www.facebook.com/valentino.capulet.5

https://www.facebook.com/angelica.angy.12327

https://www.facebook.com/magdalena.capulet

https://www.facebook.com/friar.laurence.54584

In addition to his site on Facebook, the Friar has the following sites:

Friar's site 2

http://friarlaurencesecretlab.wordpress.com

Friar's site 3

https://www.facebook.com/FriarLorenzo?ref=hl

VeronaLeaks, a Wordpress blog, informs the citizens of Verona about information withheld from public view by the city.

At https://veronaleaks.wordpress.com

The Black Mask, a mysterious, anonymous site, possibly an informant:

http://cosmoschaosandthemask.wordpress.com

Chapter 7
The Story Backgrounds

Twitterdammerung: The Twitter Opera, Prologue

900 Twitter participants—Anonymous

> It is a curious story — hear my tale,
> Although my name was never Ishmael,
> For this great epic will your souls ignite,
> Your senses ravish and your hearts deloitte...
> A story written not by one, but all,
> A composite composition to appal,
> Of passion, burning revenge and envy bitter,
> Among the gentle denizens of Twitter.
> Think, when we speak of horses, that you saw them,
> (Although in fact we couldn't quite afford them),
> The Duck of Destiny brings joys, betrayals, sins:
> The Twitter Opera approaches — It Begins!
>
> An endless opera, infinite yet uncompleted,
> The strangest tale that ever has been tweeted,
> The strangest opera ever heard or sung,
> This tragic tale of *Twitterdämmerung*...
> Long ago, in a far-off galaxy,
> a race of strange alien beings
> filled the long winter evenings
> at their computer terminals,
> interfacing like rabbits,
> on social networking websites.

© The Author(s) 2016
K. Madej, *Interactivity, Collaboration, and Authoring in Social Media*,
International Series on Computer Entertainment and Media Technology,
DOI 10.1007/978-3-319-25952-9_7

They laboured to create a new artform,
of drama, music, love, revenge and birdseed,
sung by singers of enormous artistry and weight,
a million contradictory plots
drawn from the dustbin
of the collective imagination.

After Love Comes Destruction Theme and Media: Student Suggestions

Discussion Question:
What is your main thematic interest in the Romeo and Juliet story?

Theme Descriptions

Ben
Love is a common theme in our daily life, the human kind since the beginning of the possibility of writing has talked about love, it is a feeling that brings us together, that makes us similar no matter the time or space we live in.

Love is passion and with passion comes passionate decision-making, which is something we also share. That decision making based in passion that the play Romeo and Juliet represents, could be the beginning of a social phenomena that has replied in circles, since the day the play became public, the conception of death related to love, as a possibility to escape together, could be spread by the play itself and by the poetic expression of choosing the unknown instead of the possibility of a couple being separated. References below:

http://statigr.am/tag/love

http://www.ndtv.com/article/cities/dehradun-teenage-couple-commits-suicide-by-jumping-before-speeding-train-78644

http://www.eltiempo.com/colombia/medellin/ARTICULO-WEB-NEW_NOTA_INTERIOR-11234085.html

Piper
The theme sounds fascinating to me and I think it would be worthwhile to play with the theme of conflict in Romeo and Juliet. This conflict can be related to the historical age they live in, which affects their beliefs, culture, and lifestyle and it also can show up in family conflict as well. Different beliefs, culture and family situations can affect the character relationships profoundly with their families and create some conflict for them.

Sarah

I'm mostly interested in the Communication elements of Romeo and Juliets story: but not communication as in "cell phones" or "technology" but rather communication as trying to express feelings or expectations between two people. For example: neither Juliet nor Romeo tell their parents about their relationship. Had they done so—what would the outcome have been? And how does the communication further fall apart after the couple's suicide? Do the parents communicate within their own relationship? And do the Capulet's and Montague's learn to communicate with each other? After all, the whole "war" was something neither remembered how it started. If they had communicated with one another (rather than always fighting) could they have gotten somewhere different?

I am not interested in historical or cultural context. It is important, but as seeing as this is a digital media project AND we have such little time—adding in that thick extra layer would be FAR out of scope. I much rather prefer to explore the timelessness of inter-personal relationships, and how when we, as individuals, don't communicate properly, things get misunderstood, feelings get hurt, and sometimes people die.

Nathan

My interest in exploring and using the Romeo and Juliet story in a modern (social media) context is centered around the family dynamics and how communication fits into the picture. Whether its imagining putting social media tools in the time frame that the Romeo and Juliet story was written or their story being played out today this story puts a spotlight on the family and how conflict gets resolved and the consequences or results of how they communicate with each other and then with the world outside. How an individual and/or a group of people communicate(s) with each other and others reveals a tremendous amount about their views and attitudes towards other individuals, families, communities and cultures. However, when communication methods and means are examined further a lot can be learned about how an individual or family sees and feels about themselves. But, as we move deeper into the exploration of a person or family 'psyche' we can ponder how those feelings and attitudes toward themselves were formed. Mostly though (at least in a tale such as Rome and Juliet) we can only speculate.

As we see more and more tools and techniques for communicating 'socially' through the technology of today we can't help but ask; do these tools makes us more effective in our communication? Is the technology making life better for the individual and the family?

Alexa

The main thematic interest in the story is communication. Communication is a very important skill between people and it plays a big role in each aspect of life. If we look at Romeo and Juliet in depth, we will find out that a big part of the sad ending is miscommunication and misunderstanding. The parents of Romeo and Juliet didn't communicate effectively with them which leads both of the lovers to ignore listening to their parents.

Carson
My interest in Romeo and Juliet (the project) is in the transmediation of the text and the ways intertextual narratives emerge through juxtaposition of media. The old script is being replaced by the new script and the adoption rate and form is such that we can never translate all the seeding knowledge. This leads to cloistered manipulation of (the belief in) ancient knowledge that may be hidden or exposed at will: Thematically I am interested in how the church fabricates perception to further the belief in transparency. This fabrication is traced in historical documents and found objects, spoken fragments overheard in pubs, lines of official propaganda on the evening news, bits of paper and sms messages resonating to the hidden order. The sacrifice of virginal princesses betrothed to equally sacrificial lab raised princeling rats—the clandestine attempt to breed a race of church controlled statesman, and on it goes; you're either with us, or you're with the enemy: The myths of annunciation and zombification. Resurrection myths, wars within the church, hidden and explicit wars with other churches, and the vaults full of blasphemous treasures; these mysteries that are both known and unknown, all scattered in pixels and text, ashes to dust to bits.

Audit Student
So what interests me the most about Romeo & Juliette is the social context in which they live. These two powerful families have been at feud for such a long time and it has been ingrained into their society at such a level that the state itself has to intervene to calm things down. The state is actually fearful of what the power these families wield and yet is powerless to actually stop them if they go to all out war. Placing the play in historical context, Italy in the 1500, we can relate this to the rise of the merchant class due to Mercantilism and the affront to the power of the nobles this represents. This is why the state itself, in the form of the prince, is so interested in the wedding of Romeo, as this would help appease the powerful families. This is a fascinating social context in which the love of two kids (lets face it that's what they are) can destabilize the whole city.

Audit student
The external forces surrounding the conditions in which Romeo and Juliet was written are of most interest to me as a theme. The reason being that as a writer myself, I always try and place myself in an environment that lends itself to the most proficient idea generation. Of course, this is subjective and purely personal. Certain locations, ambience, mood and space have the ability to channel influences into the work produced. I am quite curious therefore what prodded Shakespeare into the conception of the idea—was he reeling from a broken romance destined to never actualize? The potential here to generate an interesting discourse considering the external and internal forces that drove Shakespeare is quite limitless.

Discussion Question:
What social app/technology might be used to present this aspect of the story?

Social Media Descriptions

Ben
A social technology to represent this could be Vine, this new app allows sharing 6 s videos using Twitter; your family is not in there, as it is on Facebook; it is fast and easy for taking and sending videos between couples. Also has the possibility for adding hash-tags to make themes spread in a community.

Piper
Facebook (in my opinion) is the most popular social network in recent decades with more than half of the world's people supporting this media. I think Facebook is an effective way to make people more interested in taking part in creating the new story and also to give feedback and comments about this experience.

Sarah
I think Facebook is a good hub. There's lots of joke sites that use Facebook to tell the stories of fictional characters: http://www.comicsalliance.com/2009/10/05/super-social-networking-comic-book-character-Facebook-status-u/ as just one example. As Facebook has practically become the de facto log in/alliance for many auxiliary sites, such as Tumblr, Pintrest, Twitter, and Wordpress—I think we would be remiss to not utilize in some form or fashion these other sites.

Alexa
To introduce this kind of stories I find word press is suitable because multiple users can use the platform from different places at the same time. There's many options on Wordpress like having a blog, attaching power point and viewing gallery. Wordpress can be connected to other social media like Facebook that allows users to easily access it and read through Wordpress.

Carson
One friar (John perhaps) has a new cellular star, given to him by the Pontiff, that allows him access to the voices of angels; the other sticks feathers in black pools. A blend of these technologies is unavoidable. Angel wings make the best pens.

How this echoes across time—mythological time, the time of the play, the time of its author, its time in media, its timelessness in imagination may be explored in the interlinking of diverse media forms. Twitter feeds as secret notes revealing only 140 characters of a moment, codes recoded and retweeted, appropriated and mashed into an ocean of plastic. Somewhere, in the middle of the Pacific, is a polyethylene fragment of Romeo embedded in an Albatross.

We will need some form of central map. I wonder if Presi might be used as a graphic map of relationships that could lead to deeper links.

Although there's no reason why it couldn't be printed on REAL(tm) paper from the *future*.

Nathan (From Theme's Response)
As we see more and more tools and techniques for communicating 'socially' through the technology of today we can't help but ask; do these tools makes us more effective in our communication? Is the technology making life better for the individual and the family?

Audit Student
There are many ways this story can be told through, however an interesting take would be to treat these families and the state as if they were high power players in today's world. Resolving the conspiracy formed by the collusion of these players in order to stop the breakdown of society that would ensue from the shock of the death of their heirs. Using quick interactive mini-games the spectator could hack into personal emails, discover censored reports and find hidden security footage that would reveal the lengths the government took in order to ensure that peace would prevail. Maybe they killed the messenger, whose fault it is that they didn't get the message, or they're persecuting the friar who has escaped back to Rome. This thriller twist to it would allow us to give it a high-tech digital feel as we see a desperate government dealing with the fallout of these two doomed lovers.

Audit Student
Speaking as a member of the Millennium generation, growing up with all its technological revolutions and seeing the web transform the way we live—one trend has certainly manifest itself in a way that repurposes an activity that has accompanied human life for centuries. Journaling has now become blogging. Perhaps a Tumblr record of Shakespeare's influences—including videos, quotes, images and posts from other writers or creative minds? Pinterest also begins to serve that purpose well—displaying sources of inspiration that anyone can find ideas from. There could be cross pollination between various blogging, self journaling and personally reflective web apps. Elements of research, creative brainstorming, and blog writing would all be factored into the creation of this project.

Facebook Discussion: Preliminary Approach to Storyline and Character

June 5, 2013

Sarah   Hey, Romeo and Juliet group!
          So George expects us to have the semblance of a plan for our Romeo and Juliet project by tomorrow. If you guys want, we can discuss it over facebook, rather than in person?
          His questions are:
          Do the families get back together?
          Does it end with some family winning? Or still in Conflict?

Is starting voice a specific person (which George believes would be biased—which is okay) or from a choir (unbiased—and more tragedy play based)?
Where are we starting from? At what point in time—and how does it end? (What point are we moving backwards from)?
And
Are we including the City/State?

Nathan Regarding the ending: A possible ending could be what is known as a "Pyrrhic Victory" Someone who wins a Pyrrhic victory has been victorious in some way; however, the heavy toll negates any sense of achievement or profit. A "Pyrrhic victory" can also mean a false or temporary victory where a win entails a loss subsequently or in the bigger picture.
June 5, 2013 at 9:38am · Like · 1

Nathan For example, one family wins (what or how that looks I am not sure right now) But is subsequently shunned by the rest of the community…
June 5, 2013 at 9:39am · Like

Carson And my thought is that the 'resolution' itself is a perspective that shifts according to time space and character. Multiple parallel representations of the same characters make up the overlaid city of broken dreams. I think it might be interesting to not draw such tight boundaries around something called transmedia. The 'pyrrhic victory' suggests its unavoidable opposite; when is the chorus the voice of the totalitarian state, when is it the cry in the darkness? And what happened to the Vampyrric Order of Eternal Retribution? Where were they when Romeo's mom met with Juliet's dad to discuss opening a joint family gelato bar called Franco Steinellis Soft cows Emporium? Was it all the emergent fallout of a translation error in the Vatican archives?
June 5, 2013 at 12:14 pm · Like · 1

Ben The families should not get back together
June 5, 2013 at 4:36 pm · Like

Ben Conflict is something that never ends, us as humans always look for it in life.
- I vote for using the priest as the voice, using a religious videoblog channel on youtube. this is my reference: http://www.youtube.com/watch?v=PJvo7SB9TZY
- we should start from the next day they die, the first blog post could be he, being recorded while he says his good bye words, the user doesn't know who is he talking about.
June 5, 2013 at 4:41 pm · Like

Ben This show is called the "Minute of god", it is super famous in Colombia, it is a minute TV show in which a priest talk about the day, related to the bible.
June 5, 2013 at 4:44 pm · Like

Carson I vote we set up a structure, which by nature defines a set of rules, pick characters (who may be spread across time and space), and just let it evolve naturally in conversations and culture-sampling. There's no other way to write 'by committee'…
June 5, 2013 at 4:45 pm · Like

Ben Each one of us could be the perspective of a character in that case
June 5, 2013 at 4:47 pm · Like

Carson   Yes that might be easiest to manage—there could even be a few 'incidental
          characters' i.e. your perspective (your characters POV) will include persons
          and situations both known and unknown by other 'players'
          June 5, 2013 at 4:49 pm · Like
Sarah   sounds good!
          June 5, 2013 at 4:53 pm · Like
Sarah   But I think what George meant by "where does it end" is his usual shtick:
          "start from the end and go backwards from there"
          June 5, 2013 at 4:53 pm · Like
Ben   Good point, maybe we need to think in a resolution factor, after they die. A
          secondary resolution for the characters that are alive.
          June 5, 2013 at 4:55 pm · Like
Ben   The families and friends in this case
          June 5, 2013 at 4:55 pm · Like
Carson   Perhaps they had tried to get back together, put up golden statues of the kids,
          donated to the church and state, set up a hospital for the terminally Cupidic,
          introduced scholarships at the academy for the study of how the uncontrolled
          spread of Venician masked balls was undermining civil society and the morals
          of children of Rome, etc. But then it all turned to shit. Massive degeneration,
          disintegration of the state and family, the great wars, then the launching of
          angel fleets to save the world as it burns down in the abysmal hell of the
          Romeo and Juliet Effect. That kind of drift

Meeting Summary: Developing Storyline

Carson
June 6, 2013

Romeo and Juliet
What do we know?

- We have a record of Shakespeare's position.
- We know we can take different perspectives.
- Decisions have consequences over time.
- We can't change the known facts.

The 'obvious' option seems to be that:

1. The Capulet's win; the story is told from their perspective.
2. Total disintegration; Nurse and priest elope. This foregrounds the end
   condition.

An option:

Benvolio is a spy (a turncoat interested only in his own ascension to power)—
Romeo's successor if Romeo is eliminated ("you need a good traitor", a twist
perhaps where Benvolio is working both sides). "The secret weapon".

Themes:

- Family
- Communication
- Societal Context
- Love story

Media relationships?

- Friar (religion) = letters? email
- Nurse (social welfare) = tweets, FB
- Parent's (corporations) = web sites
- Prince (the law) = wikileaks, QR codes (encryption as gamification of narrative)
- Benvolio (politics) = found excerpts from Shakespeare by contemporary scholar, fake FB personality

Establish these points:

1. We need to understand the split up of the families.
2. The Capulet victory—the Prince is curious about this, leading to investigation, perhaps revealing a clue to the Prince's involvement in the deaths.
3. Benvolio as turncoat.
4. Prince's negotiations with the Capulets (reveal of the behind story of the Caps).
5. Monatgue Corporation is bought out (loses).
6. Final teaser. Benvolio takes over (discovers truth about Prince).

(Carson's view) gangster theme is a kind of 'Tarantino meets the internet')

FOR NEXT WEDNESDAY AT 9 pm:

- Flow chart and timeline—who's reporting on what?
- Show when reports enter the timeline.

Suggested requirements:

- eight posts per stream (four story months in bi-weekly postings) on company web sites.
- The nurse just babbles (about the family split-up, her involvement in the romance set-up, etc. Is she who she says she is?)
- Prince (monthly official reports to the state, to the public, communications to the church).
- The Prince and Friar Laurence would have (historically) likely been inseparable. The way that the Prince asks questions will reveal more about the Prince, his involvement and his motivations.
- In story planning always ask, "what does this get you"—what are the consequences, advantages and problems with a plot decision.

Timeline

This time line includes only the events mentioned in this book.

BCE	
2100 circa	*Epic of Gilgamesh* is written down
760 circa	Homer writes down the collectively authored mythic histories of the Greek people, *Iliad* and *Odyssey*
370 circa	Socrates writes *Phaedrus* in which Plato decries writing
CE	
300 circa	Hosidius Geta writes the earliest known Virgilian Cento *Medea*
1241 circa	*Decretals of Gregory*, glossae ordinariae shows dialogue in manuscripts
1250	Matthew Paris includes volvelle that determines changing lunar date at Easter in *Chronica Majora*
1305	Ramon Llull includes volvelles in *Ars Magna* as a mechanical means of generating theological truths
1455	Gutenberg uses moveable type to print the 42-line bible
1474	Johannes Mueller includes volvelle in his printed book *Kalendar* to compute events such as eclipses
1524	Johan Stoeffler uses lift-the-flap moveables in *Elucidatio Fabricae ususque astrolabii,* his treatises on mathematics, astronomy, and astrology
1591 circa	Pietro Bertelli introduces moveables that were socially inspired in his lift-the-flap image *Cortigiana Veneza (Venetian Courtesan)*
1597	Receipts for teams of three or more playrights evidence collaborative writing for plays
1651	Georg Philipp Harsdörffer creates a poetic volvelle, the *Denckring or Five-fold Thought-ring*
1693	John Locke writes *Some Thoughts on Education* and advocates enjoyable learning
1717	Actor Manager John Rich introduces Panto to the British theatre
1719	Daniel Defoe writes *Robinson Crusoe*

(continued)

© The Author(s) 2016
K. Madej, *Interactivity, Collaboration, and Authoring in Social Media*,
International Series on Computer Entertainment and Media Technology,
DOI 10.1007/978-3-319-25952-9

(continued)

1765	Printer Robert Sayer creates the first harlequinades
1790s	Paper dolls are introduced in books
1810	Samuel and Joseph Fuller begin publishing their *Paper Figure Adventures* such as *The History and Adventures of Little Henry*
1837	Charles Dickens completes 20th installment of *The Pickwick Papers*
1844	Alexander Dumas completes 139th installment of *The Count of Monte Cristo*
1851	Harriet Beecher Stowe writes *Uncle Tom's Cabin* (40 installments)
1856 circa	Thomas Dean incorporates pop-ups in his new series *New Scenic Books*
1860	Thomas Dean begins to publish pull-tab books such as *The Royal Punch and Judy*
1907	*Mutt and Jeff* newspaper comic appears as strip sequence
1914	*Perils of Pauline* film series started
1915	Movies are no longer produced without scripts but by production teams
1936	Henry Luce buys *Life Magazine* and changes its emphasis from weekly news to photojournalism
1944	Vannevar Bush writes *As We May Think* for the Atlantic Monthly
1962	McLuhan publishes *The Gutenberg Galaxy*
1962	Steve Russell, Peter Samson, Wayne Witaenem, Martin Graetz develop *Spacewars* on the PDP-1
1962– 1964	Joseph Weizenbaum writes *ELIZA* program at MIT Artificial Intelligence Lab
1965	Ted Nelson works with Dr. Andries van Dam to develop first hypertext-based system, coins term hypertext at ACM conference
1965	MIT implements its email system MAILBOX
1967	Marshall McLuhan discusses *The Medium is the Message*
1968	Doug Engelbart demos NLS system that provides tools for collaboration in computer environment in *The Mother of All Demos*
1968	Julia Kristeva introduces Mikhail Bakhtin's work to the western world with her translation of his work into French
1968– 1970	Terry Winograd develops *SHRDLU*, an early AI language system at MIT
1969	ARPA funds a project to network computers. The network, ARPANET, becomes the basis for the Internet
1969	Will Packard writes *The Adventures of You on Sugarcane Island,* the first interactive adventure book. It was published in 1976 by Vermont Crossroads Press
1970	Ted Nelson creates interactive catalogue *Labyrinth* for the *Software* exhibit in New York
1971	Project Gutenberg gets a life
1972	Italo Calvino writes the novel *Invisible Cities*
1973	Talkomatic, the first online chat system, is created at the University of Illinois
1974	Gary Gygax and Dave Arneson develop fantasy tabletop role-playing game *Dungeons & Dragons*
1975– 1976	Will Crowther designs the first digital text adventure, *Adventure*
1977	Barthes declares *Death of the Author*
1977– 1979	David Lebling, Marc Blank, Timothy Anderson, and Bruce Daniels collaborate to write *Zork* while at MIT

(continued)

(continued)

1978	Andrew Lippman develops the first hypermedia system to create the *Aspen Movie Map*
1978	Roy Trubshaw develops the first multi-user adventure called *MUD* while a student at Essex University
1979	The first of the *Choose Your Own Adventure* books, *Cave of Time,* is published. 180 CYOA books are produced between 1979 and 1998
1979	Jean Sherrard, Larry Stone, James Winchell, and Phillip Wohlstetter start the writing collective *Invisible Seattle*
1979	*Zork* designers Marc Blank and Dave Lebling start Infocom
1980	Compuserve releases CB Simulator, a subscriber online service that facilitates chat rooms and bulletin boards
1981	Commodore introduces the VIC-20 home computer
1981	IBM introduces the personal computer (PC) with MS-DOS basic software
1982	Drexel University requires all students to own a personal computer
1982	Word Perfect is introduced
1983	Microsoft Word is introduced
1983	*Invisible Seattle Literary Computer Project* opens at Bumbershoot Arts Festival in Seattle
1983	Clair Colquitt of *Seattle Invisibles* starts the literary blog *IN.S.OMNIA*
1983	Apple introduces Lisa, the first personal computer with a graphical interface
1984	Apple replaces Lisa with Macintosh, which is faster, has a mouse, and is cheaper
1984	Hewlett Packard introduces the LaserJet laser printer
1984	Michael Joyce and Jay Bolter meet at MIT and begin to work on Storyspace, a hypertext editing system for authors
1984	Infocom publishes *The Hitchiker's Guide to the Galaxy* video game and includes "feelies" such as Peril Sensitive Sunglasses in the package
1986	Eastgate Systems begins to publish hypertext literary works using Michael Joyce's *afternoon* as a test for Storyspace
1987	HyperCard is released for Macintosh and AppleIIGS
1987	Amanda Goodenough creates first graphical hypertext, *Inigo Gets Out,* using HyperCard
1988	Graphics are added to MUDs in the Lucasfilm game *Habitat.* Graphical MUDs are later called MMORPGs
1989	Tim Berners-Lee invents the World Wide Web
1992	Robert Coover introduces students to the *Hypertext Hotel*
1992	The Mosaic browser is introduced
1993	Deena Larson publishes the hypertext *Marble Springs* and asks readers to participate in creating the story by sending her new text
1993	Graham Nelson designs Inform, a system for writing interactive fiction. Inform 7 is released in 2006
1994	Netscape Navigator released: first browser that lets average user work interactively with the Internet
1994	Kiss.com, the first online dating site, is registered in December
1994	Justin Hall starts his personal blog Links.net that he keeps as a diary for 11 years
1994	Steve Mann begins to record his daily existence non-stop on *Lifelog*
1995	Michael Joyce publishes *Victory Garden*

(continued)

(continued)

1995	trAce Online Writing Community is launched
1995	Marjorie Luesebrink begins work on the hypermedia novel *Califia* under the writing name M.J. Coverley
1995	CompuServe produces the first online live conference for Mick Jagger and the Rolling Stones
1997	Andrew Weinreich launches SixDegrees.com, the first site oriented towards social networking rather than a special interest group
1997	Jorn Barger begins to use the word weblog, which is shortened to blog in 1999
1998	William Gillespie, Scott Rettberg, Dirk Stratton and friends begin the hypertext novel *The Unknown*
1998–1999	Teri Hoskin and Sue Thomas edit the *Noon Quilt*
1999	Evan Williams and Meg Hourihan launch Blogger.com
1999	The Electronic Literature Association is established
1999	Rob Wittig writes chatroom narrative *Friday's Big Meeting*
2000	Eastgate Systems publishes the hypermedia novel *Califia*
2001	*Blue Company 2002,* an email narrative written by Scott Rettberg and Rob Wittig is performed for the first time
2002	Johanthan Abams creates Friendster.com which calculates a users connections to other users and shows their network of friends
2002	Diego Doval starts blog novel *Plan B*
2002	Rob Wittig starts fictional blog *robwit.net*
2003	Chris DeWolfe and Tom Anderson found MySpace.com. Members can now customize the look of their profiles
2003	As Belle de Jour, Brook Magnanti starts her blog *Diary of a London Call Girl*
2004	The image and video hosting website, Flickr.com, is founded
2005	Steve Chen, Chad Hurley, Jawed Karim found YouTube.com, a video sharing website
2005	Producer Ian Harper works with author Kate Pullinger to create *Inanimate Alice*
2006	Facebook.com enters the public domain after 2 years as a Harvard University network
2006	Jack Dorsey, Evan Williams, Biz Stone and Noah Glass create the microblog Twitter.com that uses short 140 character messages
2006	Larry Smith and Rachel Fershleiser launch online magazine *SMITH*
2007	David Karp founds Tumblr.com, a microblogging platform and social networking website
2008	*The Book View Café* is launched
2008	*Mad Men* Twitter accounts appear
2009	Dylan Meconis begins first interactive Twitter novel *Dame Jetsam*
2009	Ben White, who uses Twitter to create one-tweet stories, starts *Nanoism,* a Twitter fiction journal
2009	The Royal Opera House engages Twitter users in collaborating to compose *The Twitter Opera* entirely of tweets
2009	Neil Gaiman undertakes a collective Twitter fiction for the BBC that results in the fairy tale audio book *Hearts, Keys, and Puppetry*
2010	Paul Sciarra, Evan Sharp, and Ben Silbermann found Pinterest.com, an image sharing website

(continued)

(continued)

2010	Kevin Systrom and Mike Krieger launch Instagram.com, which lets users take pictures and videos, and share them on social networking platforms
2011	Stanford University students Evan Spiegel, Bobby Murphy, and Reggie Brown create Snapchat.com, a video messaging application that attaches a set time of 1–10 s for how long recipients can view images before they are deleted
2012	OD Kobe launches Pheed.com, a social networking site that includes live broadcast and pay-per-view options
2014	Grammarly publishes crowd-sourced novel *The Lonely Wish-Giver*
2015	Grammarly publishes crowd-sourced novel *Frozen by Fire*

Photo Credits

#	Image	Reference
1		Fortran punch card. Photo: Arnold Reinhold. https://commons.wikimedia.org/wiki/File:FortranCardPROJ039.agr.jpg ASUS smart phone. Pubic Domain. https://upload.wikimedia.org/wikipedia/commons/8/8a/ASUS_Mobile_ZenFone6_20141109.jpg
2		Manuscript Leaf with Marriage Scene, from *Decretals of Gregory IX*. Metropolitan Museum http://www.metmuseum.org/collection/the-collection-online/search/468476
3		Diagrams of Ramon Llull, *Figure One* https://commons.wikimedia.org/wiki/File:Ramon_Llull_-_Ars_Magna_Tree_and_Fig_1.png *Ars Magna Figure Four* http://libguides.nec.edu/content.php?pid=399520&sid=3337061
5		Raimundus Lullus, Thomas le Myésier Badische Landesbibliothek. http://www.blb-karlsruhe.de/ http://commons.wikimedia.org/wiki/File:Codex_St_Peter_Perg_92_11v.jpg
6		*Fuenffacher Denckring der Teutschen Sprache Kunstgruendig anroeisend* Beinecke Rare Book & Manuscript Library http://brbl-dl.library.yale.edu/vufind/Record/3545854
7		*Astrolabe* by Johan Stoeffler Digital Rare Book Collection Vienna University Observatory http://www.univie.ac.at/hwastro
8		Pietro Bertelli: Courtesan and Blind Cupid Heilbrunn Timeline of Art History. The Metropolitan Museum of Art http://www.metmuseum.org/toah/works-of-art/55.503.30

(continued)

© The Author(s) 2016
K. Madej, *Interactivity, Collaboration, and Authoring in Social Media*,
International Series on Computer Entertainment and Media Technology,
DOI 10.1007/978-3-319-25952-9

(continued)

#	Image	Reference
9		*Queen Mab* or *The Tricks of Harlequin* Ellen G. K. Rubin http://www.popuplady.com
10		*Beauty and the Beast* Public Domain University of North Texas Libraries, Special Collections http://www.library.unt.edu/rarebooks/exhibits/popup2/introduction.htm
11		*Moveable Book of the Royal Punch & Judy* Public Domain University of North Texas Libraries, Special Collections http://www.library.unt.edu/rarebooks/exhibits/popup2/introduction.htm
12		*The History and Adventures of Little Fanny* Ellen G. K. Rubin. http://www.popuplady.com/about01-history.shtml
13	 	*The Cave of Time* Cover Copyright Bantam. *The Cave of Time Narrative Map* Dr. Mark Sample http://www.samplereality.com/gmu/fall2008/343/wp-content/uploads/2008/09/caveoftime.jpg
14	 	*NLS Mother of All Demos* SRI International http://www.sri.com Doug Engelbart Institute http://dougengelbart.org
15–21		*Invisible Seattle Computer Literary Project (All images)* Rob Wittig http://robwit.net
22		*Victory Garden* Sampler page Eastgate Systems, Inc. http://www.eastgate.com/VG/VGStart.html
23–24		*Califia* Marjorie Coverley Luesebrink http://califia.us
25		*SHRDLU* United States Government Image https://en.wikipedia.org/wiki/File:SHRDLUs_World.gif
26		*Adventure* PDP 10 Screen https://en.wikipedia.org/wiki/Colossal_Cave_Adventure#/media/File:ADVENT_--_Crowther_Woods.png
27		*Noon Quilt* Sue Thomas http://tracearchive.ntu.ac.uk/quilt/info.htm

(continued)

(continued)

#	Image	Reference
28–29		*Inanimate Alice* Ian Harper https://www.facebook.com/InanimateAlice
30		*Friday's Big Meeting* Rob Wittig http://www.robwit.net/fbm/
31		*Twitter Opera* ROH blog http://www.roh.org.uk/news/ twitter-opera-day-2-5-the-tweets-take-us-to-the-desert
32		*Twitterdammerung* with Hannah Pedley and Andrew Slater Lloyd Davies http://www.aqamera.com
33		*Hearts, Keys, and Puppetry* Copyright 2010 BBC Audiobooks America
34–35		*Romeo and Juliet/Book of the Future* Udita Menon
36–58		*Romeo and Juliet on Facebook: After Love Comes Destruction* Micheal Auger, Alan Correa, Rebecca Nunez, Neshat Piroozan, Brett Pawson

Bibliography

A Short History of British Pantomime. (Basel English Pantomime Group, 2010), http://www.baselpanto.org/a-short-history-of-british-pantomime/. Accessed 2015

Ancient Egyptian Literature, Mysteries in stone. (2010), http://www.mysteries-in-stone.co.uk/ancient.htm. Accessed 2015

J. Abbate, *Inventing the Internet* (MIT Press, Cambridge, 2000)

R. Adams, A History of Adventure. Rick Adams, http://rickadams.org/adventure/

P. Adler, C. Heckscher, L. Prusak, Building a collaborative enterprise. Harv. Bus. Rev. **89**(7-8), 94–101, 164 (2011). https://hbr.org/2011/07/building-a-collaborative-enterprise. Accessed 2015

T. Anderson, S. Galley, *The History of Zork* (New Zork Times, Winter 1985). samizdat.cc/shelf/documents/2004/05...historyOfZork/historyOfZork.pdf. Accessed 2015

J. Arendholz, Need to put this out there (my story) – narratives in message boards, in *Narrative Revisited. Telling a Story in the Age of New Media*, ed. by C. Hoffmann (Benjamins, Amsterdam, 2010), pp. 109–142

R. Barthes, *Death of the Author. Image-Music-Text* (Hill and Wang, New York, 1997)

M. Barton, *The History of Zork* (UBM Tech, 28 June 2007). www.gamasutra.com/view/feature/1499/the_history_of_zork.php. Accessed 2015

W. Benjamin, The work of art in the age of mechanical reproduction, in *Illuminations: Essays and Reflections*, ed. by H. Arendt (Schocken, New York, 1969), pp. 217–252

J. Bercovici, Who coned 'SocialMedia'? Web pioneers compete for credit (Forbes.com, 2010), http://onforb.es/Ndf8m2. Accessed 2015

J. Bolter, *Writing Space* (Lawrence Erlbaum Associates, Hillsdale, 2001)

A. Bonime, K.C. Pohlmann, *Writing for New Media* (Wiley, New York, 1998)

V. Bonin, *Software: Information Technology: Its New Meaning for Art* (la fondation Daniel Langlois pour l'art, la science et la technologie, 2004), http://www.fondation-langlois.org/html/e/page.php?NumPage=541. Accessed 2015

J.L. Borges, Kafka and his precursors, in *Labyrinths: Selected Stories and Other Writings*, ed. by J.L. Borges (New Directions, New York, 1962), pp. 199–202

D.M. Boyd, N.B. Ellison, Social network sites: definition, history, and scholarship. J. Comput. Mediat. Commun. **13**, 210–230 (2008)

R. Brandt, Porting to the web. Upside **11**, 16–17 (1999)

H. Briceno et al., *Down From the Top of Its Game: The Story of Infocom, Inc* (MIT Press, Cambridge, 2000)

J. Bruner, *Acts of Meaning* (Harvard Universiy Press, Cambridge, 1990)

J. Bruner, Life as narrative. Soc. Res. Int. Q . **71**, 691–710 (Fall 2004)

K. Madej, *Interactivity, Collaboration, and Authoring in Social Media*,
International Series on Computer Entertainment and Media Technology,
DOI 10.1007/978-3-319-25952-9

V. Bush, As we may think, in *The New Media Reader*, ed. by N. Wardrip-Fruin, N. Montfort (MIT Press, Cambridge, 2003), pp. 35–47

I. Calvino, *Six Memos for the Next Millenium* (Vintage International, Cambridge, 1993), pp. 116–117

M. Chafkin, *How to Kill a Great Idea* (Inc.Com, 1 June 2007), http://www.inc.com/magazine/20070601/features-how-to-kill-a-great-idea.html. Accessed 2015

C. Chapman, *A Brief History of Blogging* (Web Designer Depot, 14 Mar 2014), http://www.webdesignerdepot.com/2011/03/a-brief-history-of-blogging/. Accessed 2015

J.M. Cooper (ed.), *Plato: Complete Works* (Hackett, Indianapolis, 1997)

R. Coover, *The End of Books* (The New York Times on the Web, 1992)

F. Cramer, Cominatory Poetry and Literature in the Internet (2000), http://ada.lynxlab.com/staff/steve/public/docu/lidia/docu/combinatory_poetry.pdf

W. Cyrul, Lawmaking: between discourse and legal text, in *Legislation in Context*, ed. by L.J. Wintgens (Ashgate, Farnham, 2007), pp. 43–54

G. Dalakov, History of Computers/Dreamers/Llull (2015), http://history-computer.com/Dreamers/Llull.html. Accessed 30 Jan 2015

S. DeRose, Steve DeRose's home page (2011), http://www.derose.net. Accessed 28 Aug 2011

DigitalTrends, *The History of Social Networking* (Digital Trends, 2014), http://www.digitaltrends.com/features/the-history-of-social-networking/. Accessed 2015

M.A. Doody, *The True Story of the Novel* (Rutgers University Press, New Brunswick, 1997)

J.F. Durey, The state of play and interplay in intertextuality. Style. **25**(4), 616–636 (Winter 1991)

E. Eisenstein, *The Printing Press as an Agent of Change: Communications and Cultural Transformation in Early Modern Europe* (Cambridge University Press, Cambridge, 1982)

D. Englebart, Doug Englebart Institute (2008), http://dougengelbart.org

J. Fiderio, A grand vision. Byte **13**(10), 237–244 (1988)

S.I. Fontain, S.M. Hunter, *Collaborative Writing in Composition Studies* (Thomson Wadsworth, Boston, 2006)

C. Gabbard, Embodied cognition in children: developing mental representations for action, in *The Routledge International Handbook of Young Children's Thinking and Understanding*, ed. by S. Robson, S. Quinn (Routledge – Taylor & Francis Group, Oxon, 2015), pp. 229–237

A.K. Gay, History of scripting and the screenplay (2011), http://www.screenplayology.com/content-sections/screenplay-style-use/1-1/. Accessed 15 Dec 2014

E.H. Gombrich, Moment and movement in art. J. Warburg Courtauld Inst. **27**, 293–306 (1964)

A. Goodenough, *A Few Words from Amanda Goodenough* (2007) Author archives.

M. Gravelle, A. Mustapha, C. Leroux, Volvelles, in *ArchBook: Architectures of the Book*, ed. by A. Galey (1 Dec 2012), http://drc.usask.ca/projects/archbook/volvelles.php. Accessed 2015

S. Green, Edge3: mulitmodality, dialogics and fiction, in *Proceedings of the 18 AAWP Conference*, ed. by S. Strange, K. Rozynski (Australian Association of Writing Programs, 2013), http://www98.griffith.edu.au/dspace/bitstream/handle/10072/66740/100747_1.pdf?sequence=1

D. Grigar, *Invisible Seattle Visible Again (Hastac, 2 Jan 2012)*, https://www.hastac.org/blogs/dgrigar/2012/01/02/invisible-seattle-visible-again. Accessed 2015

R. Guisepi, *Egypt and Mesopotamia Compared The Origins Of Civilizations* (2007), http://history-world.org/egypt_and_mesopotamia_compared.htm

I. Harper, *Inanimate Alice* (Interview by K. Madej) (4 Mar 2010)

P. Harris, *Sleepless in Seattle. ALT-X Where the Literati Meet the Digerati* (ALTX NETWORK, 1995), http://www.altx.com/ebr/ebr1/harris.htm. Accessed Mar 2015

O. Harris, Burroughs is a poet too, really: the poetics of minutes to go. Edinburgh Rev **114**, 24 (2005)

M. Hart, *History and Philosophy of Project Gutenberg* (1992), https://www.gutenberg.org/wiki/Gutenberg:The_History_and_Philosophy_of_Project_Gutenberg_by_Michael_Hart. Accessed 29 Dec 2014

L. Hawkes, *A Guide to the World Wide Web* (Prentice Hall, Upper Saddle River, 1998)

J. Helfand, *Reinventing the Wheel* (Princeton Architectural Press, New York, 2006)

G. Hendrix, *Choose Your Own Adventure: How the Cave of Time Taught Us to Love Interactive Entertainment*. (Slate Culture Box, The Slate Group, 18 Feb 2011), http://www.slate.com/articles/arts/culturebox/2011/02/choose_your_own_adventure.html. Accessed 2015

J. Hoskins, Agency, biography, and objects, in *Handbook of Material Culture*, ed. by C. Tilley et al. (Sage, London, 2006), pp. 74–84

D. Howard, *Social Networking 194 Success Secrets* (Emereo, Aspley, 2014)

L. Hutcheon, *A Theory of Adaptation*, 2nd edn. (Routledge, New York, 2012)

D.G. Jerz, Somewhere nearby is colossal cave: examining will Crowther's original "adventure" in code and in Kentucky. Digit. Humanit. Q. **1**(2) (2007), http://www.digitalhumanities.org/dhq/vol/001/2/000009/000009.html. Accessed Jan 2015

S. Karr, Constructions both sacred and profane: serpents, angels, and pointing fingers in renaissance books with moving parts. Yale Univ. Libr. Gaz. **78**(3/4), 101–127 (2004). http://www.jstor.org/stable/40859568. Accessed 2015

C. Keep, T. McLaughlin, R. Palmer. *Ted Nelson and Xanadu. The Electronic Labyrinth* (1993), http://www2.iath.virginia.edu/elab/hfl0155.html

C. Knappet, *Thinking Through Material Culture: An Interdisciplinary Perspective* (University of Pennsylvania Press, Philidelphia, 2005)

J. Kornblum, *Teens Hang Out at MySpace* (USA Today, 1 Aug 2006), http://usatoday30.usatoday.com/tech/news/2006-01-08-myspace-teens_x.htm. Accessed 2015

R. Koskimaa, Visual structuring of hyperfiction narratives, in *Electronic Book Review* (Institute for the Humanities, Winter 97–98), http://www.altx.com/ebr/ebr6/6koskimaa/6koski.htm. Accessed 2015

M. Languis, T. Sanders, S. Tipps (eds.), *Brain & Learning: Directions in Early Childhood Education* (National Association for the Education of Young Children, Washington, DC, 1980)

S. Laningham, *developerWorks Interviews: Tim Berner-Lees* (IBM developerWorks, Aug 2006), http://www.ibm.com/developerworks/podcast/dwi/cm-int082206txt.html. Accessed 2015

P.D. Lebling, M.S. Blank, T.A. Anderson, Zork: a computerized fantasy simulation game. IEEE Comput. **12**(4) (1979)

J. Lessard, Adventure before adventure games: a new look at Crowther and Woods's seminal program, in *Games and Culture*, ed. by T. Krzywinska, vol. 8 (Sage, London, 2013), pp. 119–135

M. Leusebrink, *ePublishing Conference* Atlanta, GA (2002) (interview by K. Madej)

J. Locke, *Modern History Sourcebook: John Locke (1632–1704): Some Thoughts Concerning Education, 1692*, ed. by P. Halsall (Fordham University, 1996), http://legacy.fordham.edu/halsall/mod/1692locke-education.asp. Accessed 2015

S. Lodge, *Chooseco Embarks on Its Own Adventure* (Publishers Weekly, 17 Jan 2007), http://www.publishersweekly.com/pw/by-topic/childrens/childrens-book-news/article/209-chooseco-embarks-on-its-own-adventure.html. Accessed 2015

K.S. Madej, *Digital Narrative + Technology: A Symbiotic Evolution*, Research Report (Simon Fraser University, Vancouver, 2002)

K. Madej, *Characteristics of Early Narrative Experience: Connecting Print and Digital Game*. Dissertation, Simon Fraser University, Burnaby, 2007

A. Maisel, *Doug Engelbart: Father of the Mouse* (SuperKids, Educational Software Review, 11 July 2001), http://www.superkids.com/aweb/pages/features/mouse/mouse.html. Accessed 2015

S. Mann, Wearable computing: a first step toward personal imaging. IEEE Comput. **30**(2) (1997)

J. McClellan, *How to Write a Blog-Buster* (Guardian News and Media Limited, 8 Apr 2004), http://www.theguardian.com/technology/2004/apr/08/weblogs.onlinesupplement. Accessed 2015

M. McLuhan, *The Gutenberg Galaxy* (University of Toronto Press, Toronto, 1962)

G. McMillan, *#TwitterFiction: Endless Possibilities in 140 Characters or Less* (Time Books, 2012), http://entertainment.time.com/2012/12/05/twitterfiction-endless-possibilities-in-140-characters-or-less/. Accessed 5 Dec 2012

N. Montfort, *Twisty Little Passages: An Approach to Interactive Fiction* (MIT Press, Cambridge, 2005)

N. Montfort, Riddle machines: the history and nature of interactive fiction, in *A Companion to Digital Literary Studies*, ed. by S. Schreibman, R. Siemens (Blackwell, Oxford, 2008)

G.S. Morson, C. Emerson, *Mikhail Bakhtin: Creation of a Prosaics* (Stanford University Press, Stanford, 1990)

S. Moulthrop, *A Subjective Chronology of Cybertext, Hypertext, and Electronic Writing* (2002), http://web.archive.org/web/19990202111426/http:/raven.ubalt.edu/staff/moulthrop/chrono. html. Accessed 2014

P.H. Muir, *Children's Books of Yesterday*. Exhibition Catalogue (London May 1946) National Book League (Great Britain) (Singing Tree Press, Detroit, 1970)

J. Murray, *Hamlet on the Holodeck* (Simon and Schuster, New York, 1997)

J. Neilsen, *Hypertext '87 Trip Report* (2002), http://www.useit.com/papers/tripreports/ht87.html. Accessed 28 Aug 2002

T. Nelson, N. Woodman, Labyrinth: an interactive catalogue, in *SOFTWARE, an Exhibition*, ed. by J. Burnham (The Smithsonian Institute, Washington, DC, 1970)

K. Ohannessian, *Neil Gaiman, the BBC, and 124 Twitterers Make Fiction* (Fast Company, 3 Dec 2009), http://www.fastcompany.com/1475513/neil-gaiman-bbc-and-124-twitterers-make-fiction. Accessed 2015

W. Ong, *Orality and Literacy* (Routledge, New York, 2002)

S. Otto, *'The Twitter Opera': New Royal Opera House Production in 'Tweets'* (Telegraph Media Group, 10 Aug 2009), http://www.telegraph.co.uk/technology/twitter/6004758/The-Twitter-Opera-new-Royal-Opera-House-production-in-tweets.html. Accessed 2015

B.S. Palmieri, "8vo." *An Introduction to Paper Computers* (2012), https://eightvo.wordpress. com/2012/06/25/an-introduction-to-paper-computers/. Accessed Dec 2014

I. Peter, *The History of Email* (2004), http://www.nethistory.info

PRNewswire, *Mick Jagger in Live, WorldWide Conference on Compuserve* (PR Newswire Association LLC, 19 Mar 1995), http://www.thefreelibrary.com/MICK+JAGGER+IN+LIVE% 2c+WORLDWIDE+CONFERENCE+ON+COMPUSERVE-a017830626. Accessed 2015

B. Rauschenbach, History of Internet dating (Lovesites Online, 2008), http://www.lovesites.com/ tag/eharmony-history

S. Rettberg, All together now: collective knowledge, collective narratives, and architectures of participation, in *Digital Arts and Culture 2005 Conference* (Copenhagen, 2005)

H. Richter, *Dada: Art and Anti-art* (Henry N. Abrams, Inc., New York, 1965). Trans. by David Britt

E.G. Rossi, <<*Software*>> *at the Jewish Museum* (Arshake, 2013), http://www.arshake.com/en/ software-at-the-jewish-museum/. Accessed 2015

M. Rudin, From Hemingway to Twitterature: the short and shorter of it. J. Electr. Publ. **14**(2) (Fall 2011)

C. Russo, The concept of agency in objects, in *Material Worlds* (Joukowsky Institute Classroom, 7 Feb 2007), http://proteus.brown.edu/materialworlds/1825. Accessed 2015

W. Shakespeare, in *Edward III*, ed. by G. Melchiori (Cambridge University Press, Cambridge, 1998)

L. Smith, R. Fershleiser. *The Joy of Six* (PowellsBooks.blog, 2010), http://www.powells.com/blog/ original-essays/the-joy-of-six-by-larry-smith-and-rachel-fershleiser/. Accessed 29 Jan 2010

Theatre Britain, *About Panto* (2015), http://theatre-britain.com/About%20Panto.html. Accessed 2015

C. Tilley, Ethnography and material culture, in *Handbook of Ethnography*, ed. by P. Atkinson et al. (Sage, London, 2001), pp. 258–272

W.A. Trettien, *Fünffacher Denckring der Teutschen Sprache* (Electronic Literature Directory, 2 July 2010), http://directory.eliterature.org/node/574. Accessed 2015

S. Turkle, How computers change the way we think. Chron. High. Educ. **50**, 26 (2004)

B.S. Turner, *Max Weber: From History to Modernity* (Routledge, London, 1992)

T. Tzara, *An Introduction to Dada* (Wittenborn Schultz, New York, 1951)

S. Waldman, *The Best of British Blogging* (The Guardian, 2003), http://www.theguardian.com/media/2003/dec/18/newmedia. Accessed 18 Dec 2003

H. Waldrop, Invisible Seattle: a novel idea. PC Magazine. **4**(6), 198–202 (3 Apr 1984)

N. Ward, *Shrdlu* (Encyclopedia of Cognitive Science, Nature Publishing Group, 2002), http://www.cs.utep.edu/nigel/papers/shrdlu.pdf. Accessed 2015

N. Wardrip-Fruin, As we may think introduction, in *New Media Reader*, ed. by N. Wardrip-Fruin, N. Montfort (MIT Press, Cambridge, 2003)

J. Watson, *Ancient Egyptian Symbolism, The Forms and Functions* (2013), http://www.touregypt.net/featurestories/symbolism2.htm#ixzz3SyXIEhgG. Accessed 2013

I. Watt, *The Rise of the Novel* (University of California, Berkeley, 1957)

J. Weizenbaum, ELIZA—a computer program for the study of natural language communication between man and machine. Commun. ACM **9**(1), 36–45 (1966)

C.H. Whitman, *Homer and the Heroic Tradition* (Harvard University Press, Cambridge, 1958)

T. Winograd, *Procedures as a Representation for Data in a Computer Program for Understanding Natural Language* (MIT Press, Cambridge, 1971)

T. Winograd, *SHRDLU* (2014), http://hci.stanford.edu/winograd/shrdlu/. Accessed Dec 2014

R. Wittig, *Invisible Rendezvous: Connection and Collaboration in the New Landscape of Electronic Writing* (Wesleyan University Press, Hanover, 1994)

J. Zweig, Ars Combinatoria. *Art J* (Fall 1997), http://www.janetzweig.com/zweig.ars-combinatoria.pdf. Accessed 2015

Index

© The Author(s) 2016
K. Madej, *Interactivity, Collaboration, and Authoring in Social Media*,
International Series on Computer Entertainment and Media Technology,
DOI 10.1007/978-3-319-25952-9